DATE DUE

FEB 25 1994	
MAR 3 0 1994	
APR 25 1994	
NOV 0 6 1995	

Affirmation and Denial

Affirmation and Denial

Construction of Femininity on Indian Television

PRABHA KRISHNAN
ANITA DIGHE

Sage Publications
New Delhi • Newbury Park • London

First published in 1990 by

Sage Publications India Pvt Ltd
32 M-Block Market, Greater Kailash I
New Delhi 110 048

Sage Publications Inc
2111 West Hillcrest Drive
Newbury Park, California 91320

Sage Publications Ltd
28 Banner Street
London EC1Y 8QE

Published by Tejeshwar Singh for Sage Publications India Pvt Ltd, photo-typeset by Mudra Typesetters, Pondicherry, and printed at Chaman Offset Printers, Delhi.

ISBN 0–8039–9643–8 (US–HB)   81–7036–184–2 (India–HB)
0–8039–9644–6 (US–PB)   81–7036–186–0 (India–PB)

Contents

Foreword

In August 1986, the International Association for Mass Communication Research held an international seminar in New Delhi. In many ways, this seminar provided an impetus to the present study, for the salient findings of the study were first presented during that meeting. The advantage of doing so was that it served to highlight that the findings of the Indian study, by and large, corroborated the findings of media studies done on this issue in other countries, particularly of the West. But this experience also showed that very little analytical work had been done with regard to women's images on television, not only in India but in some of the countries in the region as well. In this respect, this study could be regarded as breaking new ground.

This study makes a serious attempt to decode women's images on television and to further our theoretical understanding on this issue. Its relevance could be manifold. To the professional researcher, the eclectic approach of the research methodology would be of considerable interest. To the media practitioner, the analysis of women's images on television would serve to show how one's attitudes, biases and prejudices surreptitiously surface in the production process. To the layperson, the study would highlight how a passive onslaught of television images can be dangerous and that what is needed is critical viewing and analysis so that the insidious influence of television on attitude formation, particularly of our children, can be averted.

The study was undertaken with the hope that its findings would be discussed, debated, and taken note of by the media policy-makers, planners and practitioners. While it would be premature to expect policy changes on the basis of one study, what is certainly hoped for is that the study will generate considerable interest among media researchers so that more such analytical studies are undertaken across the country. The Council for Social Development has had a history of initiating research studies that eventually influence policy decisions. If the present study is able to achieve such policy decisions, the Council for Social Development would regard this as no mean achievement.

19 September 1989   **Prodipto Roy**
Executive Chairman
Council for Social Development

Acknowledgements

This study would not have been possible but for the assistance received from several individuals and agencies. Firstly, I would like to express my gratitude to Ms C.P. Sujaya, Joint Secretary, Department of Women & Child Development, Ministry of Human Resource Development, Government of India, New Delhi, for having sponsored the present study. I am also grateful to Ms Geeta Verma, Project Officer, Education, UNICEF ROSCA, who not only expressed interest in the study but also expedited its funding so as to enable us to present the highlights of this study at a meeting of the International Association for Mass Communication Research held in New Delhi in August 1986. I would also like to thank Ms S. Gururaja, Project Officer, Women's Development Section, and Ms Razia Ismail, Regional Information Officer, UNICEF ROSCA, for their guidance and support. Thanks are also due to Dr Prodipto Roy, Executive Chairman, Council for Social Development and Dr Shib K. Mitra, Research Director, for having been supportive of our work and for having provided the necessary encouragement.

Dr Binod Agrawal, Scientist, ISRO, was the Consultant to the study and provided us with valuable intellectual support. Ms Prabha Krishnan and Ms Poornima Rao had a dual task to perform—to work as Consultants, and at the same time be involved in various aspects of the study. Poornima Rao was involved in the original design of the study, in the data collection work as well as in the production of the video programme based on some aspects of the study. She was also responsible for some of the analysis work and for writing part of the section that describes the main findings on *TV Fiction and Cinema*. My heartfelt gratitude is due to her.

Shri O.P. Misra, Director, Administration, Council for Social

Development, and Shri Tilak Raj, Accounts Officer, extended the necessary administrative support. Shri B.S. Nagi, EDP Coordinator, provided the necessary assistance with computer analysis work and Shri A.P. Rai and Shri R.S. Pandey helped in coding some of the data. My sincere thanks are due to all of them.

Lastly, my thanks are due to Ms Rita Khurana, Ms Madhur Saxena and Shri Balbir Mishra for having typed the draft report.

30 September 1989   **Anita Dighe**
Project Director

1

Introduction

A global review of the various research studies on the media portrayal of women undertaken upto 1980, stated that

> A consistent picture emerges from those research studies which have investigated the media's portrayal of women. At the very best, the portrayal is narrow; at worst, it is unrealistic, demeaning and damaging (Gallagher, 1981).

Women's problematic relationships with the communication media—their lack of access, control, under-representation and marginalisation—have been part of UNESCO's enquiries for a number of years. But while the volume of research commissioned and published by UNESCO on women and communication issues upto 1980 was slight and occasional, there has been an acceleration of research efforts after 1980 as 'more emphasis was placed on the provision of summaries, syntheses and reference materials' (*Communication in the Service of Women*, 1985). An initial review of the work titled *Mass Media: The Image, Role and Social Conditions of Women* (1979), undertaken by Ceulemans and Fauconnier, was followed by a comprehensive study *Unequal Opportunities: The Case of Women and the Media* by Gallagher in 1981.

According to Ceulemans and Fauconnier, analyses of the available literature on women and media indicated that 'media images tended to define women within the narrow confines of her traditional domestic roles and her sexual appeal to man.' This two-dimensional image was not sufficiently counteracted by alternative portrayals of women that reflected their significant contribution in contemporary society. The other major observation was that there was a disproportionate volume of research evidence available on the media image and the status of Western, particularly American, women. In other words, lacunae in the research effort insofar as women and media issues in the developing countries are concerned, were clearly discernible.

On the other hand, Gallagher has shown that the depiction of women in mass media is remarkably consistent throughout the world. Barring media controlled by governments with a strong commitment to social change, the overall picture highlighted the negative features of media treatment of women. These included 'media under-representation of women and women's concerns; the use of women as a commodity in advertising; an ambivalent attitude to women evident in certain stereotyped images in which women were exclusively and unalterably "good" and "pure" or definitely and unchangeably "bad" and "immoral".' (Gallagher 1983).

An annotated bibliography brought out by Signiorielli (1986) reviewed most, if not all, relevant articles published through 1984. The most striking revelation of this bibliography was the overall similarity and stability of the research findings. According to this document, study after study revealed that as far as media content was concerned, men outnumbered women by two or three to one; in addition, women were generally younger than the men and were cast in very traditional and stereotypical roles.

That the situation has not altered substantially is apparent from the report prepared for the end-of-decade conference held in Nairobi in 1985. One conclusion of the report was that 'the years 1980–85 were not characterised by any radical change in the communication media in relation to women's portrayal and participation' (*Communication in the Service of Women*, 1985).

Another conclusion reached in the same report related to the importance of ideology:

> . . . although the importance of structures is still clear, it seems that the strength of ideology itself was perhaps underestimated. It has been normal to suppose, for example that in societies undergoing revolutionary socio-cultural change, genuine equality between the sexes would be more easily guaranteed. Experience suggests that this conclusion is becoming less and less obvious.

As for special policies and guidelines requiring media to promote the advancement of women in member states, the UNESCO report found that only half of the 95 member states had formulated any such policies and that their effectiveness was either debatable or yet to be evaluated. Less than half the countries surveyed had carried out any research on women and media content, while globally, very little was known about women's employment in media industries.

As a response to the growing volume of criticism directed at television programming with respect to women's concerns, a number of countries have set up committees and commissions to intervene on behalf of women citizens. For example, the Canadian Radio-Television and Telecommunications Commission (CRTC) established a task force on sex-role stereotyping in the broadcast media. In 1982 they gave broadcasters two years to implement voluntary guidelines for non-sexist portrayals. Williams (1986) hypothesised that meaningful change would be noticed in television programming by the end of 1985, and her research on sex roles on Canadian and US television was designed to reveal this.

Her study showed, however, that although there were some minor changes in the portrayal of women, the Canadian and US television networks were still fundamentally conservative and traditional with regard to sex-role portrayals. 'Males still predominated on all networks and almost all the people portrayed as powerful, authoritative and knowledgeable were male' (Williams, 1986).

Some recent research studies have thrown light on specific areas of concern as, for instance, women in development. Steeves (1986) contends that just as women-in-development literature has failed to emphasise development communication, so the theoretical literature of development communication has failed to consider gender. The study focuses on the complementary goals of feminism, communication and development in the context of East Africa. Meier's study (1986) examined the depiction of female and male characters in Dutch television drama, especially in their relationship to power. The preliminary findings showed that although in the fictional world of television, men still hold the better professional positions, there was an interesting trend which showed that female characters were more powerful and were striving for equality than was the case in traditional drama series. According to Zoonen (1986), the conventional notion that news content would change if the number of women journalists/producers increased, was not supported by empirical evidence. She claimed that the existence of sex and power differences must be recognised and given a regular place in research questions about news production and news content.

On the Indian scene, we found a multitude of articles and papers on the relationship between women and media. The Working Group on Software for Doordarshan, set up in 1982, published its report in 1985. Popularly known as the Joshi Committee Report, it contains a chapter on women and the media. It condemns television's heavy reliance on feature films and film-related programmes, emphasising the middle-class orientation of the programme output and the near-eclipse of working class women. The Working Group recommended that women's dimensions should be integral to programming rather than be limited only to women's programmes, and that the heavy dependence on commercial films should be reduced. Other recommendations stressed content focus on existing women's groups and struggles, significant contributions of women poets and artists, grass-roots organisations, and the like.

The Audience Research Units of Doordarshan and the Indian Space Research Organisation have, from time to time, produced various impact studies, such as *Women, Television and Rural Development: An Evaluation Study of SITE in a Rajasthan Village*, 1980; *Report of a Sample Survey on Morning Transmission and Ghar Parivar*, 1979; *Women's Lives and Television as a Medium for Development: An Impact Study*, 1980; and *Report on the Survey on* Ghare Baire, 1979, etc. etc.

Chandiram and Agrawal (1982) note that, in general, women characters continue to be portrayed in an inferior position relative to men. In this assymetrical relationship, the 'wife and other' image is predominant. They further add that there seems to be a tendency to construct a pan-Indian character of women, which is difficult to identify with any one region of India. A study of women viewers in Madras city (Krishnaswamy 1986) pointed out that the respondents felt women's programmes to be superficial in their treatment of various issues. Some respondents appreciated the inclusion of 'male concerns' in women's programmes, like the one on male impotency. Others felt that women were aware of their own plight and that such programmes should be addressed to men.

Joshi (1986), who studied the participation of women at the higher decision-making levels of Doordarshan, reported that of his respondents, a large number of women felt that increasing the proportion of women employees in the structure would improve programme quality and bring about a more balanced perspective.

But in general, as the UNESCO survey has shown, very little is known about women and communication in the developing world. The area is thus wide open to both empirical and theoretical work.

The Problem

The interaction between women and television, as we have seen, has thrown up several issues of interest to researchers. The most commonly researched theme is that of disparity between women's actual lives and that shown on the medium. Thus, concern has been expressed at the elision of working class women. Similarly, researchers have expressed their reservations about the occupational roles most often depicted on television. Even middle class women are almost invariably shown as revelling in housework. There is also concern about the entrenchment of the autonomy differential between women and men through television programmes. Many researchers have voiced their anguish over the inclusion of violence and sex in programmes, and their effects on child viewers.

In the case of children, television plays an important role in their socialisation: it arbitrates in matters of attitudes, values, culture, ethics and so on. Unlike books, parents and teachers have little say in the matter of what children view on television. Children generally do not restrict themselves to programmes designed for them, but become indiscriminate viewers of programmes that insidiously influence them. It therefore becomes important to examine the stereotypical notions of gender roles presented to children both in programmes specifically intended for them as well as in general programmes.

The debate on the need for special programmes for women as opposed to the integration of women's concerns into all aspects of programming continues unabated. The rationale for special programmes for women is that they cater to the specific needs of women, and that they can be structured and timed in order to draw their attention and ensure their maximum involvement.

In order to ascertain how women are projected through the television programmes, it was considered important to critically look at not only the special programmes meant for them but also at the general programmes which are presumed to be of marginal interest to women. For instance, if an industrial gas leak is the most debated topic of the day, what is the coverage given to it by women's programmes?

Or, are women's programmes during this period concentrating on stitching rompers and on cooking recipes?

Even if women are shown as being concerned or involved, what is the quality of their participation? If inflation is in the news and is being analysed in the current affairs programmes, are at least some women economists asked their opinion? Are at least some women asked about their impressions on the effect of inflation on national prospects, international trade and the like? Or, is their involvement with inflation seen and shown as being limited only to their household budget? If an ecological disaster is being debated, are women shown only as victims or are they shown as active participants, as designers, as architects, as scientists? In other words, it was felt that such an analysis would focus on women's role expectations as portrayed in sectoral and general television programmes. Unfortunately, while descriptive analyses of television programmes have been attempted on a limited basis, no systematic quantitative study of this aspect of television programmes has been undertaken.

The present study therefore aims to provide a systematic understanding about the manner in which women and their concerns were projected through the television medium, particularly through Delhi Doordarshan. The rationale for restricting the study to Delhi Doordarshan was that the transmitter at Delhi not only caters to a population of 19 million (8.8 million urban and 10.2 million rural), but has 186 LPTs and HPTs linked with it. Since more than 50 per cent of the programmes are produced from the Delhi production kendra (*Television in India*, 1985) and the outreach of the national programmes, which begin at 8.40 p.m. every evening, is the entire country, Delhi Doordarshan would provide a fair indication of what the country as a whole was viewing.

Theoretical Context

The field of communication studies has been in a state of ferment for some time now. The initial approach to communications was based on the relatively simple paradigm of the transfer of a message from the source to the receiver. According to White, this marked the early phase of mass media studies during which there was an intuitive belief that the media could shape opinion, mould behaviour and even serve as a panacea for a host of individual and social problems. Over the years, the inadequacies of this paradigm led to a new 'receiver-centred' paradigm in which the emphasis shifted to interacting individuals together creating meaning. Culture was regarded as an important intervening variable between the source and individual effects. During the 1960s, the importance of structural factors was underscored as American and European researchers started questioning the supposedly benign intentions of mass media and began interpreting media messages as exploitative ideologies of elites. 'For them, patterns of communication and media organization were inherent in a given social structure and thus change could not be effected simply by changing the messages of powerful media but required a more equitable distribution of social power' (White 1983).

A basic premise underlying several approaches to the role of mass media in national cultures was that the media constitute the main instrument of ruling elites for maintaining ideological control. According to this Marxist orientation, the mass media are a means of social control whereby the ideology of the capitalist class is promoted in order to maintain status quo and inhibit class consciousness among the proletariat. The Marxists believe that all knowledge and art, including mass media content, are formed in the super-structure of society and that super-structure is conditioned by the mode of production (the economic and material base).

Gramsci (Simon, 1982) saw media as being embedded in what he called the 'civil society' and proposed his theory of hegemony to explain the relations between classes and their reciprocal interaction with media. Hegemony, according to Gramsci, is the organisation of consent. Whereas for Lenin hegemony was a strategy to acquire power, for Gramsci it was a tool to understand society. A hegemonic class, or part of a class, gains consent of other classes and social forces through creating and maintaining a system of alliances by means of political and ideological struggle. An important concept related to hegemony is that of the national, collective, popular will. A class wishing to establish hegemony should not only concentrate on its own class interests but take into account popular, democratic demands and struggles of the people which do not have a purely class character, that is, which do not arise directly out of systems of production. Such struggles may be related to civil liberties, national liberation movements, and movements for empowering women.

Two other concepts related to hegemony are those of the civil society, as mentioned before, and commonsense. Commonsense is used by Gramsci to indicate the uncritical and largely unconscious way in which a person perceives the world. It is often confused and contradictory and is compounded of folklore, myths and popular experience. The civil society, of which media, the church, the family, etc. are parts, is the scene of class and popular democratic struggles, and is the sphere where hegemony is exercised. Organisations comprising the civil society all embody social practices which are associated with the assumptions and values which people accept, often unconsciously. Activities designed to change the spontaneous consent given by the masses to the hegemonial class are political and the movement for women's empowerment is political in this sense. The media, which acts as the cultural arm of the state, and which revives components of commonsense such as folklore and myths, is an important bulwark of spontaneous consent and as such the locus of a great deal of feminist scholarship.

The traditional method of media analysis is that of content analysis, wherein the manifest content of the message is regarded as the most important area for scientific-social analysis. Typically, in content analysis, certain conceptual categories are established by the analysts in relation to media content and the presence or absence of these categories is then quantitatively assessed with varying degrees of sophistication. While content analysis is very useful for a systematic investigation of a wide range of material, its shortcoming is that it is not concerned with questions of quality, of responses or of inter- pretation. Janus (1977) notes that the results of content analysis need to be interpreted with care, otherwise they may well lead to the 'males versus females' perspective, in which all males are counted together as a general category, which is then contrasted with a all-female category without reference to class, race or cultural divisions. Instead, subjects are to be distinguished on the basis of visible, personal traits, such as marital status and age, which to Janus are both apolitical and ahistorical.

Content analysis as a methodology implicitly influences the kinds of questions asked and it is possible that the conclusions drawn may work against feminist interests. This is because content analysis cannot distinguish between levels of meaning—a woman newsreader talking about 'militant, bra-burning feminists' is on par with another talking about the 'feminists' reasonable case for abortion on demand'

Fiske and Hartley (1985), who agree with this view, add that 'content analysis does not help us with matters of interpretation nor with how we respond to the complex significance and subtleties of television text. That sort of reading of television requires that we move beyond the strictly objective and quantitative methods of content analysis and into newer and less explored discipline of semiotics'.

Semiotics or semiology, the science of signs, is concerned primarily with how meaning is generated in 'texts' (films, television programmes and other works of art). 'It deals with what signs are and how they function' (Berger 1982). According to Fiske and Hartley, the central concerns of semiology are two: the relationship between a sign and its meaning, and the way signs are combined into codes. Codes are highly complex patterns of associations which are learnt in a given society and culture. As Eco (1972) puts it, 'Codes and subcodes are applied to the message in the light of a general framework of cultural references, which constitutes the receivers' patrimony of knowledge, his ideological, ethical, religious standpoint, his psychological attitudes, his tastes, his value systems etc.' Fiske and Hartley have suggested that television performs a 'bardic function' operating as a mediator of language, producing messages not 'according to the internal demands of the text', 'nor of the individual communicator' but 'according to the needs of the culture' (Fiske and Hartley, 1985).

The work of theorists such as Eco and Barthes suggests that there is a tension in semiology between the analysis of signifying systems such as the mass media as internally and logically structured and the search for underlying structures. 'It is in this area that semiology becomes vitally concerned with ideology. The theoretical alliance of semiology and Marxism in the study of the mass media has produced the argument that the underlying structure is that of "myth" or ideology' (Woollacott, 1982). Barthes and Fiske and Hartley highlight the dominant class ideology of the mass media. The distinguishing feature of Barthes' analysis of media messages is the identification of second-order meanings, meanings beyond the linguistic message. According to him, these operate upon us in a manner which suppresses and conceals their ideological function because they appear to record rather than to transform or signify. Fiske and Hartley maintain that television 'responds with a predominance of messages which propagate and represent the dominant class ideology. The bardic mediator tends to articulate the negotiated central concerns of its culture, with only limited and often over-mediated references to the ideologies, beliefs, habits of thought and definitions of the situation which obtain in groups which are for one reason or another peripheral.'

Studies on gender in the field of mass communication have been done mainly from feminist–liberal and Marxist–feminist perspectives (Janus, 1977 and Sayers, 1982). According to these perspectives, society organises itself according to expectations about the place men and women should occupy in keeping with their biological functions. The social regulation of these functions has restricted women to the domestic sphere whereas it has facilitated men's participation in the public sphere. The feminist–liberal and Marxist–feminist paradigms connect this sexual segregation in the mass media's image representation to the socio-economic sphere. Socialist-feminist theory, relying on both Marxism and structuralism, emphasises the importance of equity between genders in all spheres of activities, traditional and non-traditional, private and public. Liberal feminism, on the other hand, emphasises the increasing movement of women into non-traditional roles. Socialist-feminists assume that media and popular culture perpetuate and develop cultural ideology, and if women's status is to improve, these structures must change. They further argue that transforming mass media and popular culture can make a difference even in the absence of a socialist revolution. In this they differ from Marxist–feminists who believe that change in women's status is predicated on changes in the economic structure of the state (Steeves, 1986).

The feminist perspective, Baehr (1981) notes, has shifted the crucial debate in media studies from the ideological role of the media in capitalist society to a discussion of the construction of women's exploitation and subordination, materially and ideologically, within patriarchy. Media is seen as a system of representation, a point of production of definitions. Because these are cultural questions, a cultural reading (decoding) is necessary to understand this. Following this, feminists can move towards alternative modes of media production and distribution.

A cultural reading of media messages is possible because feminist scholars study diverse social constructions of femaleness in order to understand the universal phenomenon of male dominance (Green and Kahn, 1985). They quote Simone de Beauvoir (1952) that 'one is not born but rather one becomes a woman . . . it is civilisation as a whole that produces this creature'. This conception thus becomes the central assumption of feminist scholarship which undertakes to deconstruct the social construction of gender and the cultural paradigms that support it. Feminist criticism of media then attends to the processes by which the work of gender ideology is done. Barrett (1980) lists these processes as 'stereotyping, compensation, collusion and recuperation'.

A significant body of work exists in the field of feminist film criticism. During the first stage of this work, criticism focused on the disparity between women's representation in cinema and their actual lives. Later, the very notion of woman as 'image' came to be questioned: it was felt that the media do not 'reflect' or 'distort'; rather, there exists a dialectical relationship between media and culture, which together construct the notion of 'woman'. The basic assumption of feminist film theory is that cinema is obsessed with polarities of masculine and feminine. Further work in this field led to the notion that for feminist scholars to accept conventions such as narrative/plot/hero/heroine and then to criticise sexist content or the credibility of women, is to overlook the way femininity is constructed by these forms and practices. According to Baehr (1981), narrative, genre, lighting, mis-en-scene and the like work together to construct images and their meaning. She goes on to add that such aesthetic structures and media practices in the patriarchal discourse are central problems for women. Using concepts like 'conditioning' and 'falsification' oversimplify women's complex relationship to media and the processes involved in their representation.

Given our present location within a patriarchal society, for us the crucial question becomes—how are media images and representations of femininity constructed within patriarchal social and sexual relations of production and reproduction? How can one change without a corresponding change in the other? (Baehr, 1981).

The complexity of the interaction between women and the media may arise from the production of self-consciousness by media and society. Feminist film criticism based on psychoanalysis credits the Lacanian construct of the 'look'. Keohane and Gelphi (1982) distinguished between three levels of women's self-consciousness—feminine, female and feminist.

The feminine self-consciousness sees the female body as the object of another's attention. As Berger (1972) puts it, 'Men look at women. Women watch themselves being looked at. The surveyor of women in herself is male: the surveyed, female. Thus she turns herself into an object—and most particularly, an object of vision: a sight.' The woman holding this consciousness of herself is defined by the male gaze, construct and desire. She is typically the sex object of masculinist pornography.

Mayne (1985) quoted Laura Mulvey (1975) on the power of the male gaze. 'In a world ordered by sexual imbalance, pleasure in looking has been split between active/male and passive/female. The determining male gaze projects its phantasy on to the female figure which is styled accordingly'. Even when this female figure is embodying abstractions such as dawn, peace, justice or motherland, the aesthetics of the male gaze prevail; these qualities are depicted in the form of well-fleshed young women.

In the Indian context, the feminine and the female categories as distinguished by Keohane and Gelphi blur and merge. For though the dutiful wife and mother-earth archetype belong to the female category, yet in addition to their nurturing services, they have to provide visual pleasure.

The female self-consciousness is less inert, but still at the service of patriarchy—giving and preserving life, nurturing and sustaining. She is either politically powerless and emotionally passive or imbued with mythic powers. But she is never self-defined. The feminist self-consciousness, on the other hand, reflects the assymetries of power, opportunity and situations in women's experience. This consciousness draws attention to the pervasive patterns of women's subordination, limitation and confinement in society. It goes further to envision alternate, non-oppressive ways of living. This view is entirely self-defined.

What are the analytical categories that feminists use? Harding (1986), arguing that such analytical categories should be unstable because society is unstable and incoherent, points out that analytical tools like liberal political theory, Marxism, psychoanalysis, functionalism, structuralism, deconstructionism and the like both do and do not apply to women and gender relations. This is because women's experiences have *neither* provided the grounding for any of these, *nor* generated problems which these theories attempt to resolve, *nor* have they served as a test of adequacy for any of them. Aspects or components of all are usable if these limitations are kept in mind.

Harding goes on to add that feminist enquiry should not substitute one gender loyalty with another, but work towards the transcendence of gender. She rejects male notions of dispassionate objectivity and validates women's lived experience. In this, feminist philosophy comes close to the Indian philosophy of *dwaita*, which holds that both the ego and non-ego are real in their distinction and opposition. According to this philosophy, we are never conscious of anything beyond our own consciousness of phenomena, whether they be objective or subjective. Thought and being are so inextricably united that to separate them would be to mount on one's own shoulders. Matter cannot be known per se; it can be known only through phenomena perceived by the mind. This concept is important for our consideration of reality and realism, both of which are crucial to the study of media.

A moot point to raise at this juncture is, how are the three kinds of consciousness developed? There are three main psychological theories of development which seem to elucidate how a child acquires sex-appropriate preferences, skills, personality attributes and behaviour. These are typically referred to in psychoanalytic theory, social learning theory and cognitive developmental theory. There is a fourth theory of sex-typing that has recently been introduced in psychological litera-ture—the gender schema theory. 'Gender schema theory proposes that sex typing derives in large measure from gender-schematic processing, from a generalized readiness on the part of the child to encode and to organize information—including information about the self—according to the culture, definitions of maleness and femaleness' (Bem, 1983). While at one level, the theory proposes that sex-typing is mediated by the child's own cognitive processing, at another level it assumes that sex-typing is a learned phenomenon and hence neither inevitable nor unmodifiable.

This study was designed to examine the kind of consciousness—feminine, female, feminist—that was constructed on Indian television. We hypothesise that the hegemonial process within Indian society serves to entrench patriarchy, and that the media as an organisation within the 'civil society' resonates with patriarchal ideology. In order to consolidate a national–popular collective will, the ruling class takes note of women's struggles for empowerment. Mechanisms for con-tainment now exist at the level of the state within 'civil society' in the form of organisations and as segments of mainstream media. We see feminist scholarship in the field of media as an attempt to decode and decipher 'myths' and promote critical analysis of media content so as to disrupt the hegemonial process.

Objectives of the Study

The broad objective of the study was to examine the content of television programmes in relation to women. The specific objectives were·

1. To understand what were considered women's concerns on television;
2. To examine how women and their concerns were reflected in sectoral and general programmes;
3. To investigate the manner in which sectoral programmes for women reflected or did not reflect issues of national and international concern; and
4. To ascertain the patterns of women's representation in TV programmes in terms of the functions they performed and the roles they played.

Analysis of TV Programmes—An Eclectic Approach

As noted in our discussion of theoretical considerations, the traditional approach of content analysis does not produce a complete picture of television programming. It was necessary, therefore, to supplement it with elements of structural analysis. This combination of approaches became particularly necessary since we decided to include all TV programmes, irrespective of their format, content and duration, in the sample. This led to our using semiologic analysis in order to understand how meaning was generated and conveyed through the various television programmes.

As analytical tools, we used content analysis, semiology, structuralism and the like, with all their potentials and shortcomings. We have attempted not only immanent criticism but, wherever possible, transcendent criticism of various media texts.

While content analysis was sparingly used and that, too, mainly for the analysis of TV news, its aim was two-fold. First, it was used to establish a quantitative base for more qualitative analysis of the message. Second, it helped us to categorise TV programmes according to content in a way not based on any prior assumptions or empirical categories previously applied to the depiction of women in mass media. Three researchers watched TV programmes consistently for one month in order to ascertain the patterns of programme structure. Constant interaction and discussion enabled them to evolve a common perspective. This exercise also enabled them to categorise programmes and to evolve analysis sheets in order to study them. Seven different analysis sheets were designed to analyse seven different categories of TV programmes. These analysis sheets were piloted over a one-week period of TV viewing, then modified and finalised. Thereafter, one master sheet for each programme was constructed on the basis of the sheets filled in by the three individual researchers. Each analysis sheet was discussed and debated until a consensus was reached.

Sample Size

The total sample consisted of every alternate day of Delhi Doordarshan programmes over a one-month period (July 1986). The researchers watched TV programmes that

1. Start at 6 p.m. on weekdays and continue up to 11–11.15 p.m. every night;
2. Begin at 1.45 p.m. on Saturday and continue up to 4 p.m. and later continue from 6 p.m. to 11–11.15 p.m.; and
3. Begin at 9.30 a.m. on Sunday and continue all through the day, evening and late evening.

Every single programme (inclusive of commercials) over a total of 15 days became part of the sample. However, the day-time educational broadcasts aimed at school and college students and the one- or two-minute 'fillers' and continuity programmes were not included in the sample.

2

Analysis and Findings

Analysis of TV Programmes

The TV programmes were divided into seven broad content categories on the basis of the following operational definitions:

1. *News programmes*: These were defined as programmes in which the emphasis was on reporting current events without going into analytical details. The news bulletins in English and Hindi fell into this category.

2. *Sectoral programmes for special interest groups*: These programmes were intended to reach specific categories of population, depending upon their specific characteristics and needs. They were meant to cater to the special needs of these groups in terms of content, timing, level of information, etc. Programmes such as *Bachhon ke liye, Mahilaon ke liye, Ghar Bahar, Krishi Darshan, Gramin Yuvakon ke liye, Gramin Mahilaon ke liye*, etc. belonged to this category.

3. *Enrichment programmes*: These were programmes in which information and educational components predominated. Their objective was to enable viewers to learn more about where, why, and how of products, processes, places and people. Besides the 'how-to' programmes, information-based programmes such as *Gharelu Nuske, Kanooni Salah, Jan Hai Jahan Hai, Bazm, Patrika, Vikas ki Aur* and *Beyond Tomorrow*, were also included in this category.

4. *Art and entertainment programmes*: These programmes contained an element of fantasy, fun, relaxation, etc., and made no overt attempt to provide information. Folk dances, dance-dramas, sports events, *Sugam Sangeet*, choral singing, *Chitrahaar, Chitramala* fell in this category.

5. *T.V. fiction and cinema*: These were defined as those programmes which made an attempt to reflect social realities and through entertainment, enable viewers to accept, absorb or question that reality. All TV serials and plays, as well as the weekly feature films, fell in this category.

6. *Commercials*: These included all the advertisements on TV that influenced and promoted the sale and consumption of products and services.

7. *Audience contact programmes*: These comprised two programmes. *Aap aur Hum* and *Janvani*, in which an attempt was made to establish a two-way communication and to elicit audience views.

All the TV programmes during the sample period were classified on the basis of these categories. Table 1 gives their frequency distribution.

Table 1

Number of Programmes Sampled (by category)

News	Sectoral	General enrichment	Art and entertainment	TV fiction and cinema	Commercials	Audience contact
30	31	55	33	27	186	3

News

The content categories shown in Table 2 were used to analyse every single news item contained in the news bulletins. The news items were also categorised on the basis of the location of the news, that is, the origin of the news at state, national, bi-national and international levels. The Hindi news telecast at 8.40 p.m. and the English news at 9.30 p.m. every evening, were included in the sample. Table 2 shows that there was preponderance of political news (45 per cent) over all other news items. This was true at all levels—state, national, bi-national and international. After political news, the next important news category at the state level was 'deaths and disasters'. At the international level, however, after political news, it was mainly sports that got the highest coverage.

Table 2

News Content by Coverage (per cent)

		Location			Total
	State	National	Bi-national	International	
Political affairs	13.5	8.9	8.3	14.3	45.0
Economic affairs	0.8	4.8	1.5	0.7	7.8
Human resources development	2.0	2.0	0.4	0.0	4.5
Infrastructural development	4.5	5.5	0.7	0.3	10.9
Health	0.5	0.1	0.0	0.1	0.8
Law and order	2.3	0.7	0.0	0.4	3.4
Deaths and disasters	5.7	2.9	0.4	2.3	11.3
Religious affairs	1.0	0.1	0.0	0.0	1.1
Art, entertainment, culture, sports	1.9	1.9	2.6	6.1	12.7
Science and technology	0.8	0.8	0.3	0.3	2.2
TOTAL	33.3	27.7	14.2	24.6	100

While news was regarded as a 'structured' programme with fixed positions for certain news items such as sports and weather, it was considered necessary to rank the first ten news items for each day's news to ascertain which items got precedence over the others. The analysis showed that political news once again assumed a higher position over other news items. In the case of the main Hindi and English news, political news constituted 66 per cent and 66.3 per cent respectively of the first ten news items.

How did women fare in the news bulletins? On the whole, men were newsmakers in 77.4 per cent of the cases, while women were newsmakers in 6.5 per cent of the cases (14.9 per cent were unspecified). The overwhelming visibility of men in the news as opposed to an almost negligible presence of women newsmakers is comparable to the findings of other research studies enumerated by Ceulemans and Fauconnier.

In every instance where men were newsmakers, they featured for a mean time of 52.0 seconds whereas women did so for a mean time of 41.2 seconds. Table 3 shows the content categories in which men and women were newsmakers. Men were predominant in the area of political affairs (40.3 per cent). As political leaders—statesmen, heads of government—they figured in the news that originated at the state, national, bi-national and international levels. There was a distinct celebrity orientation to the news as well-known personalities were newsmakers in 60 per cent of all the news items. Women politicians featured as newsmakers in political news emanating at international levels as, for instance, in news relating to Margaret Thatcher and Corazon Aquino. As ministers at the national level, women were newsmakers as they inaugurated seminars, conferences and presided over meetings. They also made news in the sports arena at the international level. The fact remains, however, that women as newsmakers constituted a very small percentage.

On the other hand, women were reported/mentioned/seen in 25 per cent of the cases. Because of the celebrity orientation of the news and the tendency for the cameras to follow political leaders, women invariably figured in political news as wives, mothers or daughters of well-known leaders. They also appeared frequently as members of audiences and as victims of some calamity or accident. A significant number of them appeared as shoppers. This was because during the sample period, curfew was imposed in various cities and was relaxed only to allow women to shop for the family. As part of development news in the weekend news bulletins, women featured as workers in tea plantations, sericulture, poultry farming and so on. They were also shown as beneficiaries of different welfare schemes.

In terms of mean time, women, when reported about, featured for 70.5 seconds. This longer exposure compared to their presence as newsmakers is due to their occupying the same frame as the men who were the newsmakers.

Questions were asked regarding the type of visual support provided for the news. We attempted to find out whether the cameras actually went out into the field, as well as establish whether there were pictures, film clips and other visual support for the news. Table 5 shows that, by and large, news items had no visual support. When support was provided, it was in the form of a film clip or a still picture. Considering the celebrity orientation of the news and the fact that men were newsmakers mainly in the area of political affairs, it was but natural for the cameras to go into the field to cover male political leaders.

There appeared to be a marked tendency to use the voice of the newsreader rather than of protagonist in the news (in at least 91.8 per cent of the cases).

Table 3

Men and Women as Newsmakers (by content category) (per cent)

	State M	State F	State U	National M	National F	National U	Bi-national M	Bi-national F	Bi-national U	International M	International F	International U	Total M	Total F	Total U
Political affairs	11.3 (82)	—	1.9 (14)	8.7 (63)	0.1 (1)	0.1 (1)	8.0 (58)	—	—	12.3 (89)	1.2 (9)	0.8 (6)	40.3 (292)	1.3 (10)	2.9 (21)
Economic affairs	0.7 (5)	—	0.1 (1)	4.0 (29)	0.2 (2)	0.5 (4)	1.2 (9)	—	0.2 (2)	0.2 (2)	0.1 (1)	0.2 (2)	6.2 (45)	0.4 (3)	1.2 (9)
Human resources development	2.0 (15)	—	—	1.1 (8)	0.1 (1)	0.6 (5)	0.4 (3)	—	—	—	—	—	3.5 (26)	0.1 (1)	0.6 (5)
Infrastructural development	2.6 (19)	0.4 (3)	1.5 (11)	3.5 (26)	0.8 (6)	1.1 (8)	0.6 (5)	—	—	0.1 (1)	0.1 (1)	—	7.0 (51)	1.3 (10)	2.6 (19)
Health	0.4 (3)	0.1 (1)	—	0.1 (1)	—	—	—	—	—	—	—	0.1 (1)	0.5 (4)	0.1 (1)	0.1 (1)
Law and order	1.6 (12)	0.1 (1)	0.5 (4)	0.6 (5)	—	—	—	—	—	0.1 (1)	—	0.2 (2)	2.4 (18)	0.1 (1)	0.8 (6)
Deaths and disasters	3.3 (24)	0.4 (3)	1.9 (14)	2.2 (16)	0.1 (1)	0.5 (4)	0.2 (2)	—	0.1 (1)	1.1 (8)	0.4 (3)	0.8 (6)	6.8 (50)	0.9 (7)	3.4 (25)
Religious affairs	0.5 (4)	—	0.4 (3)	0.1 (1)	—	—	—	—	—	—	—	—	0.6 (5)	—	0.4 (3)
Art, entertainment, culture, sports	0.9 (7)	0.1 (1)	0.6 (5)	1.2 (9)	0.2 (2)	0.4 (3)	2.0 (15)	0.4 (3)	0.1 (1)	4.4 (32)	1.2 (9)	0.5 (4)	8.7 (63)	2.0 (15)	1.9 (14)
Science and technology	0.5 (4)	0.0 (2)	0.2 (2)	0.8 (6)	—	0.1 (1)	0.1 (1)	—	0.1 (1)	0.1 (1)	—	0.1 (1)	1.6 (12)	—	0.5 (4)

Table 4

How were Women Reported (Per cent)

Categories	Location				Total
	State	*National*	*Bi-national*	*International*	
Political affairs	10.5	7.2	7.7	16.0	41.4
Economic affairs	0.6	3.3	0.6	0.6	5.0
Human resources development	2.8	2.8	0.0	0.0	5.5
Infrastructural development	5.5	7.2	0.0	0.6	13.3
Health	1.7	0.0	0.0	0.0	1.7
Law and order	1.1	0.0	0.0	1.1	2.2
Deaths and disasters	5.0	3.9	0.0	3.3	12.2
Religious affairs	1.1	0.0	0.0	0.0	1.1
Art, entertainment, culture, sports	1.1	3.3	1.7	8.8	15.5
Science and technology	1.1	1.1	0.0	0.0	2.2
TOTAL	30.4	28.7	9.9	30.4	100

Table 5

Whether News was Field-based (per cent)

	Male	*Female*	*Unspecified*
No	46.7	3.8	9.6
	(343)	(28)	(71)
Yes	30.5	2.7	5.0
	(224)	(20)	(37)

Sectoral Programmes

These programmes were intended to reach specific categories of population, depending on their specific characteristics and needs. The underlying assumption of these programmes was that they catered to the special needs of these groups in terms of content, timing and level of information. Programmes such as *Bachhon ke liye, Mahilaon ke liye, Ghar Bahar, Gramin Yuvakon ke liye, Krishi Darshan* and *Anganwadi* belonged to this category. The sample included 31 programmes ranging from 15 minutes to 30 minutes in duration. Except for Sunday, sectoral programmes appear on all days of the week.

Sponsorship

All the nine programmes for farmers were sponsored by firms such as Hindustan Machine Tools, Eicher Good Earth and Shriram Fertilizers and Chemicals. None of the children and youth programmes were sponsored, while women's programmes were only occasionally sponsored.

Format

The greatest variation in format was seen in the programmes for children and youth. There were three quiz programmes, one animation film, three documentaries, one magazine programme, and one programme of song and dance, apart from interviews and talk shows. The majority of women's and farmers' programmes were interview-based.

Content

The children's programmes in the sample covered two quizzes on general knowledge, sports, Indian music and dance; how rain is made; documentaries on the Moscow state circus and on athletics for children (both imported programmes); learning the alphabet; folk song about the rains; Rajasthani dance; exhibits in the National Museum of History; a demonstration on making and flying aeromodels; and party games.

The youth programmes dealt with such topics as the National Integration Camp held in Delhi, career guidance for graduates (opportunities in public sector units) and a dance competition in Welham Girls School, Dehra Dun.

The farmers programmes in the sample covered topics like the cultivation of oilseeds (featured twice), vegetables, trees, paddy, flowers and small grains. There was also information on other farm activities such as soil and water analysis, crop insurance schemes, care of farm machinery and the application of fertilisers and pesticides. Viewers were offered information on infrastructural support to the agricultural sector, such as import of plants suitable for Indian conditions, rural energy development, weather forecasts and crop insurance schemes for loan recipients in Rajasthan. Subjects like health care during monsoons and the welfare of weaker sections in Delhi were also covered.

Women's programmes covered topics such as women artists' exhibition at the National Gallery of Modern Art, fabric painting, printing as an occupation for women, hair care and recipes for the use of leftover bread. Information was also provided on technical education for self-employment, covering areas such as sewing, embroidery, shorthand, typing and so on; savings schemes in post offices, scientific storage of foodgrains, diseases due to polluted water, balanced diet during pregnancy, immunisation of children and details about the Integrated Child Development Services Programme.

Table 6

How were Men and Women Shown?

Categories	Compere		Expert		Interviewer		Participants		Audience	
	M	F	M	F	M	F	M	F	M	F
Women's programmes N = 8	—	10	4	15	—	1	—	2	—	3
Farmer's programmes N = 9	13	—	23	—	—	1	4	2	9+	4
Youth and children's programmes N = 15	5	7	8	—	—	2	13+	13+	+	+

Note: + = mass

As far as women's programmes were concerned, there was emphasis on the home as the locus of women's lives. There seemed to be an assumption on the part of the programme producers that women have ample time for leisure: hence the programmes on sewing cushion covers, preparing exotic dishes and tedious hair care processes. Fifteen women featured as experts in the women's programmes. They included several artists, two doctors, a midwife, a government official and the owner of a printing press. There were also housewives who functioned as experts demonstrating bread recipes, cushion cover embroidery, hair care and fabric painting. In addition, four males featured as experts in these programmes: two artists, one doctor and one government official.

While women's programmes included male experts, the programmes for farmers were entirely male-oriented, with no female comperes or experts. In the nine farmers' programmes sampled, some 11 women appeared—4 as entertainers, 3 as agricultural workers, 2 as housewives and 1 as an interviewee (this last was the wife of the VC of an agricultural university)—but they did not appear in any decision-making context.

In programmes catering to children and youth, women appeared as comperes in 'non-technical' areas, as for instance, in programmes which dealt with learning the alphabet, party games, etc. 'Technical topics' such as aero-modelling and sports were covered by male comperes.

There was no effort in these programmes to reflect issues pertaining to terrorism, ethnic identity and apartheid, all of which were topical during the sample period. The only programme that reflected a national/international trend was the discussion on AIDS. But here, too, the slant was on women as being responsible for family health and for community morals.

Visual Support

Only 9 of the 31 sectoral programmes were location-based; the rest were confined to the studio. Visually, support for these programmes included film clips, pictorial and textual studio graphics, and demons-trations. Once again, only the programmes for children and youth exhibited some variety in visual support, which ranged from film clips, animation, song and dance and skits, to quiz and glove puppets.

A close monitoring of these programmes revealed that such support was inadequate both in terms of use and quality. Film clips would frequently be lumped together at the beginning of the pro-gramme, and then followed by an interview with the expert. Sometimes, no reference was made to the visuals while they were being shown. This made it difficult to recall them when they were referred to later in the programme. Very often, the visuals appeared to have been put to token use: they did not supplement, complement or extend the text in any way.

The quality of the visuals, often left much to be desired. In a programme on nutrition during pregnancy it was suggested that pregnant women would benefit from fresh, locally available, seasonal foods, and that unrefined sugar and sesame seeds could help over-come nutritional anaemia, generally held to be an important indicator of health status and a grave problem in rural India. Yet the only visual used in the programme was a segment of a chart showing such vegetables as asparagus and Brussels sprouts. It is difficult to believe that the producers could not bring bananas, peanuts, spinach and gourds to the studio. On the other hand, a comparatively unimportant topic like hair care was visually well supported. Various ingredients for home-made shampoo were brought, and every stage in its preparation explained at great length.

The programme on the postal savings scheme was also inadequate in terms of visual support. A female postal employee showed the viewers various forms and cards and explained the utility of the different schemes. A visit to the post office and interviews with women savers bringing out the benefits they received as well as the difficulties they faced in various transactions would have added immensely to the appeal of the programme.

The stills used in the programme on imported plants were incomprehensible. Similarly, while showing how to cultivate azolla, a blue-green algae, for use as a fertiliser, the shot of the azolla pond in black and white only served to mystify. Very often, the stills, graphics, and studio furniture were so repetitive that one was left with a sense of *deja vu*. Sometimes, the visuals were of debatable value. In a farmer's programme, the discussion on water-borne diseases was supplemented by a visual depicting buffaloes and children bathing together in a pool of water. While it was rightly said that such a practice would help spread diseases, it was not made clear that in the absence of individual or community water supply and sanitation facilities, the rural poor had no option but to share the same body of water with the animals, and use that water for drinking and cooking as well. Instead, their ignorance of hygiene was highlighted.

This upper class orientation could also be discerned in the programme on paddy cultivation. A visual of a man operating a mechanical rice planter was used to indicate progress in the field of agricultural technology. That the use of this transplanter by men would lead to heavy displacement of female labour from this sector was not even hinted at. The obvious advantage of the machine made it apparent that it reduced the drudgery of the male farmers and glossed over the underlying play of a very different social process.

As already pointed out, though a majority of the sectoral programmes were studio-based, there were some that were shot on location, while some had components of both formats. But it is interesting to note that during the sample period, only two location-based programmes were shot outside Delhi. In both cases, the location was quite near Delhi—Hissar in one case, Dehradun in the other. Both locations were distinctly upper class: the garden of the Vice-Chancellor of Haryana Agricultural University, Hissar, and Welham Girl's School at Dehradun. In all other location-based programmes, the camera was confined to the environs of Delhi.

Adequacy of Treatment

Evaluation of the treatment meted out to the various topics in sectoral programmes was made on the basis of the language used (pace and terminology) and the level of the treatment. Except in programmes for children and youth, where often the content itself did not merit profundity, the mode of handling the subjects concerned was generally inadequate.

Very often, the programmes for farmers appeared to be overloaded with information. The pace was either too fast or the speakers too verbose. Sometimes, the Hindi used appeared to be formal and assumed a high level of technical knowledge. At other times, the treatment appeared simplistic, belabouring the obvious.

A few of the children's programmes had good comperes who neither dominated the participants nor talked down to them. Other programmes in this category, however, seemed to have missed their mark because the children appeared bored and uninvolved. The programme on learning the letters of the alphabet was too confusing for any real learning to take place. While the screen was filled with children moving haphazardly or overshadowed by large placards, the audio track was unclear.

The programme on exhibits in the National Museum of Natural History could not have added much to the viewers' store of information. There were repetitive shots of exhibits behind the glass cases, accompanied by such comments by the compere as: 'Isn't the bird beautiful?' 'Isn't the snake frightening?' 'That animal is stuffed'.

A glove puppet was used in a couple of programmes, but it was static, confined to a window sill, and tended to talk in a high-pitched voice, slurring its words. It was obvious that the producers had not fully explored its potential. At times, its comments were confusing. At one point it said it had come straight from the jungle (when it was clad in shirt and dungarees) and then talked of learning the alphabet in a school in the jungle.

The programme on the National Integration Camp was simplistic in its treatment of a difficult issue. While differences in food and dress habits were pointed out, commonalities were not stressed. The focus of the camp (and the programme) appeared to be on boys and girls from different states singing, dancing and eating together, in the hope that somehow a national identity would be forged. Questions about food and cooking were addressed only to girls and not boys while, in fact, a man was actually engaged in cooking during the conversation.

Several programmes displayed a one-sided approach. In the one on tree plantation there was no attempt to look at the problem of fuel wood used by the urban poor. They were blamed for using trees planted on roadsides and the expert spoke of 'proceedings' against them. There was also talk about the necessity of a clean environment and anti-pollution measures, without any reference to the causes of urban pollution, such as factories and automobile exhausts. In the segment on paddy cultivation, as mentioned before, the use of technology was lauded without taking into account the displacement of women it would entail.

The women's programme on Integrated Child Development Services was sketchy and superficial. The segment following, on recipes using leftover bread, was disproportionately long and detailed. Housework was glamourised and mystified and the monotony it entails, ignored.

In the programme on water-borne diseases and immunisation, both of which are important concerns for women, the structural constraints governing the use of clean water were unquestioned. Instead, women were assumed to be ignorant of basic hygiene. They were exhorted to immunise themselves and their children, as if such services were freely and routinely available.

Women were asked to go to health centres for ante-natal check-ups or routine health care, and immunisation. They were asked to use clean water for drinking and cooking. Farmers were asked to use a range of fertilisers and pesticides for their gardens and farms. The emphasis was thus more on technique and the use of better technology. There was no discussion of the fact that such services and inputs are not routinely available, and, if available, are within reach of only the prosperous segment of the population.

Comparing the women's programmes with those for farmers, we noted that the question of livelihood for women was raised only in two programmes, and at a rather superficial level at that. The programme on technical education options was a recitation of courses available. It included no interviews with participants or parents or prospective employers regarding the utility or drawbacks of those courses. The interview with the owner of a printing press did bring out some details of her life, but there was disproportionate emphasis on her home life and her adjustment to the demands of her husband and children. A certain level of available capital was taken as a given. This same programme also contained an interview with a woman who sold flowers in winter, and *jamuns* in summer. Here, too, the coverage was simplistic; it was difficult to avoid the impression that the woman's life was 'framed' for middle class viewers, much like the view from a window in a moving train. There was no attempt to go into the reasons for the woman's seasonal employment; instead the focus (as much as possible in such a brief encounter) was on how the family adjusted to the situation.

Other programmes in the women's slot were also simplistic. The *Anganwadi* programme on disease caused by polluted water and the programmes on immunisation are a case in point. Here, again, one could see an attempt at 'framing' a pretty picture—the studio set designed to resemble a rural sit-out, with a woman sitting cross-legged on a *charpoy*, a *kurta* hung on a nail, a grass mat and a *rangoli* design on the floor, and the 'rural' woman who looked thoroughly unconvincing.

All told, the choice of topics and the level of their treatment seemed to be geared to providing a simple, uninvolved glance at various issues, much like a Films Division documentary preceding an entertaining feature film. The objective was not so much to question, probe and rouse viewers to participate in solving various problems but, rather, to keep them informed, in a non-aggressive way, of 'development'.

The farmer's programmes were all related to agriculture, but appeared to be addressed to individual viewers engaged in a linear progression towards prosperity. While the landless remained wholly unaddressed, one could discern no attempt at considering cooperative farming either.

That such programmes were consciously or unconsciously targeted at prosperous segments of the population was clear when we tried to construct profiles of the viewers for whom these programmes would be most appropriate. To do this, we used a list of paired opposites. The viewer for farmers' programmes emerged as rural, prosperous, mostly landowning, familiar with technical terms and a resource creator with marketable skills. Viewers of women's programmes were generally found to be urban, prosperous, literate and formally educated, while the profile of those who watched the programmes for children and youth was urban, prosperous, literate, formally educated and familiar with English language. The scoring of the attributes on the list of paired opposites was done on the basis of a combination of factors, the most important being content of the programme.

We also attempted to describe the tone of the programmes on the basis of a list of attributes. For instance, the most frequently scored attributes for *Krishi Darshan* were 'dull', 'formal', 'patronising' and 'unequal', though one was distinctly hostile. A majority of people felt that while the tone of the women's programmes was seemingly 'informal', it was also 'one-sided' and 'patronising'. In the programmes for children and youth, the tone of discourse ranged from being 'dull' to being 'informative' or 'informal'.

Enrichment Programmes

Predominantly informative and educational in nature, the objective of these programmes was to enable viewers to learn more about the where, why and how of products, processes, places and people. They included both regular, periodical programmes such as *Kanooni Salah, Jan Hai Jahan Hai, Bazm, Patrika, Beyond Tomorrow, Focus*, etc., as well as irregular programmes such as *Flight of the Condor* and *Teleprinters*. The average duration of these programmes varied between 10 and 30 minutes.

Of the 55 programmes in this category, 37 (67.7 per cent) were periodical in nature. No discernible pattern was evident in the distribution of enrichment programmes over the sample period. Even on weekends, when entertainment programmes predominate, there were at least two enrichment programmes on Sundays; on one Sunday there were as many as five. The number of enrichment programmes increased during periods of national mourning, as was evident during the early part of the sample.

Sponsorship
Largely unsponsored, only 7 of the 55 programmes were sponsored. Of these, one was in English, 4 in Hindi, and one each in Urdu and Gurumukhi. Three of the sponsored programmes dealt with health, and one each with economic affairs, human resources development, religious affairs and literature.

Content
The content categories used for the enrichment programmes were the same as those used for coding news, with programmes constituting a large proportion (23.4 per cent).

Format
The interview format seemed to predominate: 34 programmes (61.8 per cent) of the 55 were interview-based. These were spread over all subject categories, with health accounting for 12 of them. There were several documentaries and cartoons as well.

Visual Support
The visuals used in most of the programmes consisted of film clips, although about 5 of them—2 in the health and 3 in the science category—had demonstration sequences.

How did Men and Women Feature?
A study of how men and women were featured in these programmes revealed that men overwhelmingly appeared as comperes and experts, outnumbering women in all categories.

Table 7 shows that even though health is traditionally considered to be the domain of women, males featured more often as comperes and experts (10 male comperes and 10 male experts as opposed to 3 female comperes and 5 female experts). However, programmes like *Yoga aur Swasthya, Jaan Hai Jahan Hai, Gharelu Nuske* and *Aap ka Parivar* show interesting variations in compering and the use of experts. *Yoga aur Swasthya* demonstrates yoga, hygiene and exercises, and has both male and female demonstrators. But the format it follows consists of a female compere asking questions and referring to readers' letters while a male expert provides the answers.

Gharelu Nuske deals with household remedies for common ailments. This programme has undergone some changes. In the earlier format, presented as a mini-drama, the programme was set in a household, with the grandmother shown as the repository of traditional wisdom, detailing remedies based on plant extracts, etc. In the present format, the expert on household remedies is a male and he is interviewed by a male. Very often, a third man is featured as the patient. However, nothing has been added to the programme in visual terms—no plants are brought to the studio, neither is there any demonstration on the actual preparation of any medicine. Textual

Table 7
How Men and Women Feature

Categories	Compere		Expert		Interviewee		Participant		Audience	
	M	F	M	F	M	F	M	F	M	F
Political affairs	9	—	18	—	3+	2	7+	1+	1+	1+
Economic affairs	1	—	—	—	—	—	1	—	—	—
Human resources development	8	2	11	—	24+	7	—	—	+	+
Infrastructural development	2	1	11	2	6+	8	3	0	+	+
Health	10	3	10	5	4	3	3	2	—	—
Law and order	4	—	1	1	4	3	—	—	—	—
Religious affairs	—	—	—	—	—	—	6	4	—	—
Art and entertainment	9	2	17	2	—	10	2	—	—	—
Science and technology	4	2	14+	1	2	—	—	—	—	—
TOTAL	47	10	82	11	43+	33	22	7+	1+	1+

Note: + = mass

studio graphics are inserted to show lists of ingredients and symptoms. In one programme, the compere himself was moved to comment that the discussion would have been more instructive if the doctor had brought along the necessary ingredients.

The new format is neither more instructive nor more professional in its presentation. Yet, even in the sphere of household remedies, the woman has been displaced by a male expert. Was this done in order to infuse more 'credibility' into the programme? Given the many commercials that extoll grandma's wisdom, the change seems to be a rather strange one. Advertising does not feature non-credible experts.

The third health programme, *Jaan Hai Jahan Hai*, supposedly based on the western system of health care, featured men in all three roles: comperes, experts as well as patients. Depending on the topic, *Aap ka Parivar* featured both men and women as comperes and experts. The programme on family planning methods featured female comperes and a female doctor as the expert, while in the programme on skin diseases during monsoons, both expert and compere were males. The family planning programme appeared to be directed entirely at women, holding family limitation to be their responsibility. Consequently, the discussion focused only on female contraceptive methods. Not only did the topic warrant a holistic 'family' approach, the stated audience for the programme was also the family as a whole.

Women did not feature as experts in any of the programmes dealing with human resources development. They appeared twice as comperes, but only in certain segments of the programmes. Even as interviewees, women featured less often than men. They did, however, appear *en masse* as audiences.

Art and entertainment programmes, traditionally viewed as belonging to the female domain, also featured comparatively few women (comperes: 9 males, 2 females; experts: 17 males, 2 females). Of the 10 enrichment programmes in this category, 5 dealt with literature, 2 with music, 1 with crafts, 1 with care of pets and 1 with sports. Expectedly, science and technology programmes generally considered to fall within the male domain had even fewer women (comperes: 4 males, 2 females; experts: 14+ males, 1 female).

Only 13 out of 55 programmes (23.7 per cent) were location-based. Five of them dealt with human resource development, 2 with infrastructural development, 2 with health, 1 with political affairs, 3 with science and technology and 2 with art and entertainment. Of these, at least 7 were geared to presenting only the government viewpoint.

Adequacy of Treatment

The following considerations were used to determine the adequacy of the programmes' treatment:

- What was the level of treatment? Did the programme present varied points of view or was it one-sided?
- Was the language, pace and terminology used appropriate for the topic?
- What was the tone of discourse?

Of the 55 programmes, only 23 were found to have been treated adequately. In general, there was a tendency to provide a facile, one-sided picture of various problems and situations. The tone of discourse was often propagandist. A few examples will illustrate the point. In a discussion on dowry problems, a woman magistrate who was interviewed suggested that the aggrieved woman should go to a police station or a magistrate. It might have been more appropriate if the programme had included a representative of a women's organisation who could have educated viewers about the actual difficulties likely to be encountered in this situation. Without this component, the programme lost much of its credibility.

Eight out of 9 programmes on human resource development were propagandist. In *Gyan Deep*, a young man enacted a situation concerning the educated, unemployed youth. Instead of pursuing this topic, which would have been of interest to at least three sets of viewers—villagers educated unemployed youth in general, and members of Gyan Deep Clubs elsewhere—the compere complimented the man on his grasp of Hindi. The ability of interviewees to speak Hindi was repeatedly applauded in this programme. Though interviewees often referred to the problems of the poor, the poor were seen only in the background, never interviewed.

Some of the 23 programmes that were well presented had been imported. In a UN programme, *Free Namibia*, the political position of native Namibians was clearly explained and the programme's focus on women and their concerns was well defined. Women featured as members of both groups, the oppressed and the oppressors, as investors, workers, freedom fighters and survivors. The interview with the Yugoslav Prime Minister was also competent. In *Patrika*, the interview with the actress Usha Banerjee was lively because the actress was asked to enact a piece to show how she had picked up the mannerisms of rural women.

Tone of Discourse

The tone of approximately 50 per cent of these programmes was formal, while the rest were informally structured. They were also equally divided in being informative and propagandist.

Profile of Viewers

The profile of viewers that was obtained for the different types of programmes was as follows:

Categories	Terms used
Political affairs	Urban, familiar with English, interested in domestic and international political affairs.
Economic affairs	Urban, prosperous, educated, interested in fiscal matters, landowning, English speaking.
Human resources development	Urban, educated, potential entrepreneurs, voters, those engaged in welfare and development activities.
Infrastructural development	English speaking, urban, engaged in development activities.
Health	Middle and affluent class, urban, those with access to health services, English speaking, familiar with technical terms.
Art, entertainment, culture and sports	Formally educated, urban middle class, interested in literature, arts, folk arts, music, etc.
Science and technology	Urban, educated, familiar with English language, with wide-ranging interests.

These profiles were gleaned on the basis of content, language and visuals used in the enrichment programmes with the help of semiological analysis. It is apparent from them that the programmes had a distinct class bias and were meant predominantly for an urban, educated and middle class audience.

Art and Entertainment

This was an omnibus category and included programmes of film song clips (*Chitrahaar* and *Chitramala*), classical dance and dance dramas, classical and pop music, and sports events. The break-up and the sponsorship of the 31 programmes included in this category are shown in Table 8.

Table 8

Content Categories and Sponsorship

Categories	No.	Whether Sponsored	
		Yes	No
Film song clips	5	5	—
Classical dance and dance drama	6	5	1
Classical music	13	—	13
Pop music	2	2	—
Sports*	5	4	1
	31	16	15

* Direct relays of matches such as Wimbledon, cricket, football, hockey, snooker, as well as video recordings of these were not included in this category.

Chitrahaar and Chitramala

The programmes based on film song clips featured three times a week: two of these programmes were in Hindi, and the third consisted of songs in regional languages. The latter category did not feature during the sample period. These programmes are possibly unique to Indian television, for songs are integral to Indian cinema. Jayomanne (1981) notes that within the so-called 'formula' film, songs have a crucial function to perform, since it is in songs that hopes and desires which cannot be realised are quite often expressed; the music expresses and contains the energy which the narrative is often incapable of articulating. This is certainly true of Indian cinema, and the extreme popularity of these songs is witness to the possibility that they meet a deeply-felt psychological need. The film song clip programmes on television were also very popular and were all sponsored. Since they are viewed as pure entertainment, they were not telecast during the period of national mourning which fell in the earlier part of the sample period.

Each programme consists of five to six songs drawn from feature films. In order to analyse the depiction of men and women in these songs, about 10 to 12 main themes were identified, such as man-woman romance, male bonding, family situation, violence and rape, revenge, seduction, religiosity, dignity of labour, motherhood, female togetherness, patriotism and rural development. These themes were not necessarily mutually exclusive.

Man-woman romance, in which the lovers are celebrating their togetherness, featured most often (18 times in a total of 27 songs), followed by situations where the lovers were separated and pining for each other (4 times). Other themes included family situation, religiosity, female togetherness, violence and revenge. In these songs, we noted polarities of male–female behaviour, that is, men were largely shown as aggressive and confident while women were depicted as shy and responsive to male advances. Women were also shown as worshipping their husbands, being dependent on them, competing with each other for male favours, and revelling in motherhood. The polarities extended to dreams as well. Young girls were shown dreaming of their future as brides and wives; male children, on the other hand, dreamt of their professional roles in the future.

Some songs depicted extremes of sadism and violence, and though they were often directed at other men, such displays of male strength and aggression served to intimidate women.

As has already been pointed out, songs depicting man–woman romance predominated in the sample. These were usually quite explicit in nature, often bordering on the vulgar.

Classical Dance and Dance-dramas

Of the classical dance and dance-drama programmes, 5 were sponsored. Following the precepts of the *Natya Shastras*, the depiction of women and men in classical dance programmes tended to uphold femininity and masculinity as binary opposites. Women were also shown as devotees, longing for union with the Lord. The moods expressed comprised the nine *rasas* of love, mercy, fear, and so on. Often, women were shown as ideal consorts, sharing their husbands' tasks. Men were shown as embodiments of virtue, capable of conferring salvation on their lovers.

Ideal male and female characters were presented in highly stylised form within rigidly structured situations. That is, women were ideally consorts of powerful men (usually gods) or shown as *Shakti* incarnate.

In such cases, no deviants from the ideal were shown. Ideal behaviour in men and women was rewarded by acceptance and glorification by society.

When female characters played the central role in the dance, they were invariably depicted from the masculine perspective. These women were shown as essentially feminine, that is, as beautiful women whose very existence was an aesthetic experience. By implication, they were sheltered and non-productive. Ardent and patient, they were idealised as lovers. As consorts, these women were shown as incarnations of energy, energy that was under male control. Since their very existence was mediated through male desire, separation from the beloved was presented as a human condition which created a special problem for these women. In the main, two courses of action were offered as solutions to this problem—pining away with patient acceptance until the lover returned or wily machination to cheat the other women and win back the lover.

In all these narratives, only one agent was presented as the problem solver—the male. Union with this male was depicted as the perfect end. These narratives appeared to be projecting the same message—that women without men were incomplete. They therefore had to strive in every possible way to retain their lovers.

Beauty and passivity were promoted as desirable values for women. These necessitated idle, non-productive lives, where the women strove for long hours to turn themselves into aesthetic visions. Economically and psychologically, these women were completely under male domination and were so constructed from the standpoint of the elites.

One dance-drama, cast in the modern mould, attempted to show drug addiction among the young. In it, young people turned to drugs to escape reality. Reality for the girl was boredom, for the boy joblessness. Parents were shown as being too self-centred to guide their children. The fathers were involved in their jobs, the mothers in rounds of socialising and partying. The narrative was so weakly structured that boredom was shown as a special problem for women and addiction to drugs the solution. The agent responsible for solving this problem therefore became the drug-pusher. The messages underlying this presentation were that society was degenerate, parents dysfunctional and children were addicted. Cure was possible and viewers were exhorted to face and fight difficulties rather than seek escape through drugs.

Classical Music

Programmes on classical music predominated in the sample. They were all unsponsored. Four main themes were identified in these programmes. 'Pining for love' featured most often, followed by 'religiosity', with the 'celebration of love' and 'nature' being next in line. There were two programmes of instrumental music. Lead singers and players were of both sexes, although the accompanists were invariably male.

Pop Music

There were 2 programmes of popular music and both were sponsored. Both followed the same format. Two or three singers, accompanied by an orchestra, sang singly or together for an invited audience. The singers and their songs were introduced by a compere of either sex. The themes of the songs centred mainly on 'pining for love' and the 'celebration of love'.

Sports

There were five programmes in the sample that covered sports events, and all but one were sponsored. They included quiz and sports programmes, but direct transmission and relays of single games such as cricket, tennis and snooker were not covered.

As regards format, two programmes were based on single games, two were magazine programmes and one was a quiz. Women featured largely as members of the audience, although in one game they were players. As participants in the quiz programmes, they did not volunteer a single answer. The comperes were invariably male.

Television Fiction and Cinema

Cinema has been considered together with television fiction rather than as a separate category. Of the 27 programmes that covered TV fiction and cinema, 23 were commercially sponsored. In 9 of these programmes, there was a direct relationship between the latent message of the commercials that sponsored the programmes and the text of the narrative. Analysis showed that in both commercials and fiction, there was a sharp polarisation of roles along gender lines. For instance, a serial that depicted women exclusively within the home, with men controlling the action, all the commercials that preceded it (for soap, detergent, refrigerators and after-shave lotion) reflected the same polarisation. Toilet soap commercials featuring glamorous, light-skinned women sponsored a serial for children depicting woman as a desirable princess.

Commercials for energy malt drinks featured doting mothers serving young sons and basking in the reflected glory of their sons' achievements. These went with the serial that contrasted 'feminine' girls engaged in household activity and boys and 'boyish' girls exploring the world and engaging in action. In several commercials, films and fiction programmes women were presented as being home-bound, serving man and children and seeking male approval, while men were located in the world outside. Thus, commercials served to underscore and emphasise the messages contained in the fiction programmes.

In the 27 programmes that covered TV fiction and cinema, men were principal characters in much larger numbers than women (105 principal male characters as opposed to 55 female characters). In terms of occupation, most of the women (34) were depicted as house-wives. The rest comprised stray cases of a dress designer, school teacher, flight attendant and office workers—occupations that are basically female-oriented and extensions of female roles.

In the case of male characters, however, the range of occupations represented was very wide. There were industrialists, bureaucrats, businessmen, journalists, executives, police officers, farmers, scientists and defence personnel. There appeared to be a distinct preference for 'white collar' jobs and 'blue collar' workers were seldom principal characters. The only exception was the serial *Nukkad*, in which the focus was on working class people.

We tried to describe the goals of the principal characters by ana-lysing what they said and did. The results are given in Table 9.

It is clear from Table 9 that, as in sectoral programmes, in fiction, too, the home formed the locus of women's aspirations and activities. The men were oriented to the world outside the home, and derived their successes and failures from that sphere. Thus, though both men and women appeared to seek peer group approval in large numbers, men acknowledged as peers figures from the larger world, while women drew theirs from within the home. Thirty-four men, as opposed to 5 women, sought success through individual effort, whereas 24 women, as opposed to two men, sought reflected success only through supportive action. Another important goal for men was resource creation (30 opposed to 4 women). For women, resource conservation was an important goal (8 opposed to 4 men). Men considered upward mobility more desirable

Table 9

Male and Female Goals as shown in Fiction Programmes

Goals	No. of characters	
	Male	Female
1. Begetting children, particularly sons	—	5
2. Seeking familial approval	9	21
3. Religiosity, ritual participation	2	7
4. Achieving success through individual effort	34	5
5. Achieving reflected success only through supportive action	2	24
6. Acquisition of commercial skills	3	—
7. Resource conservation	4	8
8. Self-realisation	5	—
9. Begetting sons to ensure patriliny	5	—
10. Seeking peer group approval	36	24
11. Seeking power in the outside world	48	5
12. Seeking power within the home	9	11
13. Seeking fulfilment through marriage/spouse	1	24
14. Resource creation	30	4
15. Meeting survival needs	15	14
16. Upward mobility	23	9

than women did (23 opposed to 9 women), while both seemed equally preoccupied with meeting survival needs (15 men, 14 women).

Each of the principal characters was described on the basis of a list of 88 personality attributes of polar opposites. Analysis revealed that the most common attributes that could be ascribed to the male and female characters were:

Most Common Attributes

Male characters	*Female characters*
self-centred	sacrificing
decisive	dependent
self-confident	emotional/sentimental
seeking a place in larger world	anxious to please
conniving	defining the world through family relations
dignified	maternal
dominant	

ruthless
ambitious
unprincipled
assertive
loyal

It was assumed that descriptions of ideal male and female characters, as well as descriptions of deviant male and female characters, would provide an understanding of the values that guide the behaviour of men and women. To do this we analysed the plots of the fictional programmes and cinema televised during the sample period. The analysis revealed that the ideal woman was

1. Caring, concerned, maternal,
2. supportive, she helped men achieve their goals and did not have any ambitions of her own,
3. sacrificing, empathetic, home-centred, family-oriented,
4. passive, accepted her wife/daughter-in-law role, accepted male control and ensured bonding,
5. unquestioning, naive, submissive,
6. pretty, charming, retaining essential femininity,
7. produced sons to ensure patriliny,
8. devoted to her husband no matter how oppressive he was, defended her married state and died unsullied, if abandoned, and
9. engaged in traditional rites and rituals.

A deviant woman, on the other hand, was one who

1. Dominated her husband and did not remain at home to look after comforts of the family,
2. had personal ambitions and did not further male goals,
3. did not produce sons,
4. broke up family ties,
5. disrupted male bonding, and
6. was not understanding, accomodative enough.

The ideal male was one who

1. Exhibited diligence, loyalty, thrift, courage, wisdom, obedience to elders, dignity,

2. sought adventure, challenged authority,
3. showed single-minded devotion to a calling or vocation,
4. was in control of the home, defended family honour, and
5. fought for a just cause, put country before self.

The deviant male

1. Did not care for family interests, or protect members of the family,
2. put self above community or country,
3. did not protect the weak,
4. was violent to women,
5. did not earn/provide for the family, and
6. accepted dominance of wife.

Rewards for ideal men and women and punishment for deviant men and women also differed along gender lines. Ideal women gained the approval of families, particularly their males, while deviant women were cast out or punished until they reformed. Men whether ideal or deviant, were rewarded/punished by the outside world. Thus, the idea of the home as a proper setting for females, and the world outside comprising the male sphere of operation, was relentlessly propagated by the fiction programmes.

Significant patterns emerged from the analysis of the age composition, marital status and urban or rural backgrounds of the characters that were of importance to the narrative. Fifty-seven male as against 20 female characters belonged to the age group of 40 years and above, while 29 female and 22 male characters were aged between 11 and 25 years. Thus we can see that older men dominate, for age commands authority and power, while the numerical balance tips in favour of women when it comes to the age group that is young, vulnerable or attractive.

A larger number of adult men (17) as opposed to adult women (3) had an unspecified marital status. In most cases, the woman's marital status was clearly indicated. In the fiction programmes analysed, 42 of the 69 women were portrayed as being married while 24 were single, whereas of 113 men, 50 were married and 43 were single.

Most of the fiction programmes were squarely located in an urban milieu. Among the important characters, 97 males and 61 females were urban, whereas only 16 males and 10 females were rural. Most of the characters—54 men and 50 women—belonged to the middle class. Only 29 men and 16 women were drawn from the upper class, while 23 men and 7 women came from the working class.

All fiction programmes, without exception, depicted women and men involved in activities that reflected common sex-role patterns. We tried to define these patterns by grouping the activities under categories that reflected polar opposites. Their analysis revealed that society's expectations regarding women and the roles they play were reinforced by the activities in which the fictional characters engaged.

Women were largely (*a*) home-bound, (*b*) supportive of male endeavour and decisions, (*c*) helpless in crises, (*d*) engaged in keeping the peace, (*e*) ritualistic and superstitious, (*f*) sacrificing and passive, (*g*) decorative, (*h*) shown as longing for a male child, (*i*) incomplete without man and child, (*j*) fighting over desirable males, (*k*) having no control over their own lives, (*l*) praying and fasting for husband's well-being, (*m*) accepting battering and violence (*n*) objects of consumption. When women were not depicted as being home-bound, they were shown as being the breadwinners because there was no male adult in the family. They were largely engaged in extensions of traditional female roles, had no decision-making power and were never actually shown at work. Even when they were the sole breadwinners, or earned substantial incomes they were emotionally located in the home. In one case, when both the woman and man were gifted with the same talent, the woman had to defer to the man. His career took primacy over hers. When young girls were portrayed as daring, adventurous or as capable of taking the initiative, they were invariably 'boyish' in appearance and behaviour. Again, a boyish girl was juxtaposed with a 'feminine' girl—thus providing the counterpoint that reinforces the stereotype. Female characters were also invested with another set of attributes, such as ruthlessness, jealousy and greed for material possessions and status, attributes which drive her to push the man along evil paths. Sometimes, even when female characters appeared to be engaged in a wide range of activities, these were in fact limited to a narrow spectrum of female-role expectations.

Analysis of the activities of male characters also revealed a certain pattern. Men in TV fiction were portrayed in various positions of power outside the home. They were shown as (*a*) decision-makers, (*b*) in command of situations (*c*) the prime breadwinners of the family, (*d*) influencing the course of events, (*e*) taking initiative, (*f*) authoritative, (*g*) adventurous, daring, (*h*) rescuing women in crisis situations, (*i*) single-mindedly pursuing careers/avocation, (*j*) demanding male children, (*k*) accusing and punishing 'deviant' women, (*l*) controlling women's lives (discarding wives, remarrying), or lusting after them.

Men who deviated from this pattern were usually 'weak'—the martyred victims of 'domineering' women. These men often reversed the deviant pattern at the end of the story by taking control of the situation and restoring normalcy. Sometimes, they were economically disadvantaged and thus vulnerable to victimisation by powerful men. In both cases, they elicited audience sympathy. However, there was yet another set of deviant men who were depicted as criminals, and whose actions carried the plot forward. Analysis revealed that the progression of plots was effected by 21 male and 9 female characters. Only 6 male, as opposed to 14 female characters, found it difficult to exert their will.

A matrix was drawn up to understand the nature of relationships between all principal characters. Relationships were categorised as either equal or hierarchical. It was found that 25.5 per cent of all relationships between female and male characters were equal, as were 18 per cent of the relationships between female and 17.6 per cent of the relationships between male characters.

Next, we tried to understand the nature of the hierarchical relationships and the bases or reasons underlying the domination of one character over another. The reasons were identified as (*a*) age, (*b*) occupation, education, (*c*) gender, (*d*) familial, and (*e*) personality.

While a fair degree of overlapping was found in the bases for domination, an attempt was made to identify the overriding reasons/bases. If, in a relationship between a man and a woman, the woman was older, better educated, had a better job, possessed a stronger personality and was not related to the man, the man nevertheless dominated her, this was ascribed as domination due to gender.

Table 10 shows that in the case of relationships between men, domination was largely based on age and personality differences, while in those between women, familial reasons accounted for an overwhelmingly large number of the hierarchical relationships. Women were found to dominate over men largely because of personality or familial reasons, while gender was found to be the overriding reason for the domination of men over women.

Only 7 out of the 27 cinema and fiction narratives had no equal relationships; in the rest, there were examples of equal relationships in all three categories.

Of the 22 equal relationships between men and women, 5 involved

Table 10

Relationship between Characters (per cent)

	Equal	Age	Occu-pation	Gender	Family	Person-ality	Class
M × M	6,7	9.9	6.7	—	7.6	9.4	4.5
	(15)	(22)	(15)		(17)	(21)	(10)
F × F	3.6	3.1	1.3	—	7.6	3.6	0.4
	(8)	(7)	(3)		(17)	(8)	(1)
F × M]		4.0	1.8	—	4.9	6.7	1.8
]		(9)	(4)		(11)	(15)	(4)
]	9.9						
]	(22)						
M × F]		5.8	2.2	21.6	14.8	3.6	1.8
		(13)	(5)	(48)	(33)	(8)	(4)
							100
							(220)

husbands and wives or lovers, but the reasons for the prevailing equality varied. In one case, though the serial was still in progress at the time of analysis, it appeared that husband and wife were locked equally in an unresolved conflict: neither could prevail on the other to change his or her viewpoint; neither was dependent economically or emotionally on the other. In another case of unresolved conflict, husband and wife were equally strong in their integrity and obstinacy, though in this instance they seemed to be emotionally dependent on each other.

Three narratives portrayed equality between lovers. One showed youngsters cast in the Romeo–Juliet mould. Their equality stemmed from their equal need of each other. In the second narrative, both the woman and the man were called upon to arbitrate in the lives of other people, that is, they each had the same standing in the community. While the woman was required to check the excesses of the man, the reverse was not true. This was not an indicator of the superiority of the woman, but of her weaker characterisation. The text was male-centred. The third narrative portrayed the lovers' need of each other as being of equal intensity. They were also equally stern in their chastisement of the erring mother.

In five cases, equality stemmed from the superficial characterisation of the men and women, and involved both familial and non-familial relationships. In two narratives, the parity between man and woman stemmed from their equal poverty or helplessness. In three cases, equality resulted from the common goals shared by the characters, and the equal strengths they brought to bear in the furthering of these goals. In one case, equal strengths were used in conflict.

There were only two cases where the characterisation was deliberately structured to explicate gender equality. In one, an adaptation of Louisa May Alcott's *Little Women*, a young boy and two young sisters were seen as equal in their attributes, and shown as working towards the same goals. In the other, a young freedom fighter was shown involving his wife in the struggle. She found the strength to overcome her father's objections. Other relationships of equality in this text occurred between the man and his mother, and between the mother and the wife's father.

We noted eight relationships of equality among women characters. Of these, seven occurred within the family structure, and involved pairs of sisters, pairs of sisters-in-law and two sets of daughters-in-law and mothers-in-law. Only one of these relationships was conflict-oriented. The non-familial relationship of equality occurred between a court dancer and the wife of a court singer; this relationship, too, was conflict-oriented. Among the men, we noted 14 cases of equal relationships. Of these, seven occurred within the family structures, between father and son, between brothers-in-law, and between a man and his prospective son-in-law. Equal relationships outside the family structure occurred between colleagues and collaborators on the one hand and antagonists on the other. Relationships of equality displayed both supportive and antagonistic interactions.

An attempt was also made to study the quality of interaction between principal characters in television fiction. The descriptors employed in this regard were:

1. *Supportive* was the term used to describe interactions in which characters were found to support each other in working towards their individual goals and aspirations.
2. *Antagonistic* was used to describe interactions in which characters actively worked against the fulfilment or realisation of each other's goals and aspirations.
3. *Neutral* was used to describe situations in which characters appeared to interact minimally, if at all, and in which they neither supported nor worked against the realisation of each other's goals or aspirations.

4. *Parallel* interactions were those in which the characters seemed to share the same goals and aspirations, but did not actively support each other in realising them.

Table 11

Interactions between Characters (per cent)

	Antagonistic	Supportive	Neutral	Parallel
M × F	15.8	32.0	4.7	1.1
	(53)	(107)	(16)	(4)
M and M	13.7	14.6	2.3	0.5
	(46)	(49)	(8)	(2)
F × F	4.7	8.9	0.2	0.5
	(16)	(30)	(1)	(2)
				100
				(334)

Table 11 makes it clear that TV fiction was so structured that the bulk of interactions were divided between being supportive and antagonistic. Only a few of them fell into the neutral or parallel categories. This was true irrespective of whether the interactions were between female characters, or between male characters or between females and males. However, female characters tended to be more supportive than antagonistic to one another, while male characters were found to be supportive and antagonistic in fairly equal numbers. In a large number of instances, male–female interaction also tended to be more supportive than-antagonistic.

Female characters were supportive of each other in various contexts. For example, supportive interaction occurred between members of the same family, that is between sisters, mothers and daughters and sisters-in-law. There were three instances of a supportive relationship between mothers-in-law and daughters-in-law. In one, the narrative focused on a patriotic household involved in the freedom struggle, and the freedom fighters were shown as being supportive of each other. In another, the mother-in-law was supportive of the daughter-in-law because she mistakenly thought her to be an heiress.

Supportive relationships also occurred between women even outside the family situation. In one instance, the heroine was depicted as a generous and caring person. Consequently, she was supportive of the hero's estranged wife, whose cause she championed. In another case, the relationship between the queen and maid was typically feudal while in a third case, the heroine was supported in her desperate need to know the future by a witch. In one narrative with working class protagonists, the inhabitants of a certain street were depicted as one large family and the supportive interaction between the two main female characters was sisterly and stemmed from the conscious class-lessness of the middle class professional woman *vis-a-vis* the domestic worker. In another instance, the hero's colleague sympathised with the hero's wife in her poverty and vulnerability.

In general, the supportive interaction among women stemmed from their need to further male goals, except in the case of one narrative. This narrative was overtly propagandist, seeking to establish the small-family norm. It was thus critical of the male need to ensure patriliny, particularly if it resulted in a large family. It is important to note that no woman supported another in the furtherance of her own individual goals, especially if these happened to clash with male goals. The antagonistic male-female relationships occurred when the women were unsympathetic to male goals.

Commercials

We saw roughly 186 different commercials, some of which were repeated several times during the sample period. They can be broadly divided into six product categories: (1) foods, (2) medical aids, (3) grooming aids, (4) household goods, (5) agricultural, industrial and electronic goods, and (6) public services.

Table 12

Commercials by Product Type

Product type		Percentage
1. Foods	46	24.7
2. Medical items	21	11.3
3. Grooming aids	43	23.1
4. Household goods	31	16.7
5. Agricultural, industrial and electronic goods	32	17.20
6. Public services	13	7.0
	186	100.0

As we can see, women featured in all the sub-categories and their visibility was very high. Table 13 shows the dominant figures and the actual user/s for each commercial category.

Table 13

Dominant and Actual Users

	Dominant figure(s)			Actual user(s)			
	Male	Female	Children	Male	Female	Children	General
1. Foods	11	13	10	5	11	15	19
2. Medical	13	4	3	10	2	7	2
3. Grooming	13	21	1	13	23	2	9
4. Household	5	21	—	2	22	1	4
5. Agricultural/ Industrial/ Electronic	22	3	—	17	5	1	7
6. Public services	7	5	—	2	2	5	4

A distinction was made between the dominant figure/s and actual user/s in the commercial because these two often varied. For example, in the commercial for a face cream, the dominant figure was a good-looking, fair and youthful woman. She was also the actual user of the product which made her look so tantalisingly soft and lovely that she was envied by another woman and admired by her own husband. But in the commercial for a toothpaste, while the male authoritative voice, presumably of the dentist, established the dominance of the male figure in the commercial, it was the woman who was the actual user. For she was shown to be asking questions, looking surprised and obtaining information about the benefits of the toothpaste from the all-knowing male voice.

However, it was not always easy to identify the dominant figure. For instance, in the commercial for chocolate eclairs, while two children were the actual users in that they were shown licking lollipops, both the presence of the male bear and the visual and jingle that accompanied the commercial suggested sexual overtones. Unquestionably, the dominant figure in the commercial was male.

Table 13 shows the variation between the dominant figure/s and actual user/s shown in the commercials. In some cases, it was not possible to identify any dominant figure for a commercial, in other cases, the actual users included a 'general' category. But on the whole, women tended to be dominant figures in the 'grooming', 'household goods' and 'foods' categories whereas men were dominant figures in the 'medical aids' and 'agricultural, industrial and electronic goods' categories. They were also shown as actual users in these commercials. Children figured most in the 'foods' category.

An attempt was made to list the occupations of those who featured in the commercials as well as the activities they were engaged in. Analysis revealed that either the man's occupation was unspecified, or he belonged to one of the professional categories: scientist, doctor, executive, farmer, etc. Women were featured predominantly as housewives. While the women's marital status was quite obvious by their 'mangalsutra' or wedding ring, the marital status of men could be inferred only when they were shown as part of a family. Though young women were shown sporting with young men, sipping soft drinks or hot chocolate, the older women were invariably married, located within the home and engaged in domestic chores. Single, professional women never endorsed any product—domestic or non-domestic.

The activities they engaged in varied according to the type of product that was being advertised. In the case of food products, women were engaged in cooking, serving, feeding children, or looking admiringly at the male child. In the commercials for medical aids, women were invariably shown in caring, servicing roles as they attended to adult and young males. They were hardly ever shown as actual users. In the ads for 'grooming aids', they adorned themselves, applied lotions, or used beauty soaps in a caressing, languorous manner and displayed their bodies seductively. In advertisements for household products, they washed clothes or shopped for household goods, looking contented and smug as they went around the house performing various housewifely chores.

Men's activities, on the other hand, were either of an outdoor nature or work-related as they played, exercised, lounged around, drove or rode to work as busy doctors, executives or successful farmers. In the ads relating to agricultural items, men drove tractors, broadcast fertilisers, sprayed crops and were engaged in buying and selling agricultural produce and products.

Women, on the other hand, either adorned themselves, tried on jewellery or danced around as the harvest came in. These findings corroborate those summarised by Ceulemans and Fauconnier (1979): 'Woman is utilised in advertising to sell products to both male and female consumers by virtue of her two-dimensional role: her role as housewife/mother/wife and her function as a decorative and sexual object.'

Commercials seemed to socialise children into polarities of male–female behaviour. Girls were shown imitating their mothers in domestic chores, that is, cooking, serving, washing, ironing clothes and child-minding. In the ad for Burnol cream while the mother ironed the daughter's clothes, the daughter ironed the dolls' clothes. In the commercial for Cold Rub, a young girl was seen scolding her doll for playing in the water, in much the same way that her mother scolded her. These commercials were the only two in which women were shown as users of medical aids. Young boys were shown consuming health drinks and medical products in preparation for their future professional roles or their activities in the field of sports or academics. They, too, imitated their fathers in bestowing approval on their mother's cooking. Young girls were shown admiring a pretty bride's good looks, while a young boy imitated his father by using shaving cream in a grown-up, authoritative manner.

One significant feature of the men's position of authority with regard to women was the off-camera voice-over, which is used in many commercials to summarise the virtues of the product and to validate the women's role as a discerning consumer. Table 14 shows that while the quality of the male voice-over was predominantly authoritative, the female voice-over was almost never so. Whenever female voice-over was used, its tone was either informative or seductive. This was particularly so in the case of grooming ads.

Table 14

Quality of Voice-over

	Male				Female			
	1	2	3	4	1	2	3	4
Foods	14				1		2	2
Medical	17	1		1		5	1	1
Grooming	29	2	7	1		3	10	8
Household	18		3			5	4	5
Agricultural/Industrial/ Electronic	25		1	1			2	
Public services	10	1				3		

Note: 1 = Authoritative 3 = Seductive
   2 = Informative 4 = Other

The life-styles promoted were largely elitist. In determining this, the researchers depended heavily on various signs—for instance, a large private garden, extensive domestic spaces, accessories such as a lace table-cloth or a silver tea-set, and motor vehicles like the Mercedes, etc., denoted an elite life-style. The absence of any overt signs of ostentation was regarded as promoting a middle class life-style. Special attention was paid to the skin colour and personal grooming of the people featuring in the commercial: an overwhelming number of the models were found to be light-skinned. Even where working class people were featured (for various agricultural and industrial products), they failed to convince because of their grooming and skin colour. Thus for agricultural and industrial products, the accent was on the rural elite. Elite life-styles were heavily promoted in ads for foods (36 out of 46 ads), grooming (30 out of 43 ads) and in agricultural/industrial products (8 out of 8 ads).

The latent messages of the commercials were invariably more demeaning and enfeebling to women than were the manifest messages. These messages urged women to enhance their *appeal* to men or gain their *approval* by using the product concerned. Many messages acted as *role reinforcements* for young boys and girls—for example, in an ad for a cooking medium, a little girl imitated her mother in seeking the approval of the males, while a little boy imitated his father in *approving* the females. The fourth category of messages bolstered *extremes of gender-specific behaviour,* i.e., macho men or possessed women.

In 24 out of 46 ads for foods, women sought male approval. In 17 out of 43 ads for grooming products, women sought to appeal (sexually) to men. In this category, 18 out of 43 ads promoted male and female polarities. In 5 out of 10 ads for vehicles, women sought to appeal to men, while all 10 promoted gender polarities. In ads for grooming products, a heavy use of sexual symbols could be discerned. These could be observed in the accompanying lyrics and statements, camera movement (caressing and often voyueristic), clothing and so on.

Most public service commercials did not have latent messages. In the agricultural/industrial category, all 8 ads promoted gender polarities. They generally showed men as being resource generators and women as resource consumers.

Audience Contact

Three programmes of *Aap aur Hum* were broadcast during the

Table 15

Life-styles and Latent Messages

Categories	Life-style		Latent messages			
	1	2	1	2	3	4
Foods	8	36	2	24	6	2
Medical	8	10	3	13	4	11
Grooming	13	30	17	7	1	18
Household	19	11	—	25	4	5
Agricultural/Industrial Electronic/ Electric/Vehicles	9	18	9	6	4	24
Public services	9	2	—	3	1	4

Notes: *Life-style*: 1 = Middle class   2 = Elite
Latent messages: 1 = Appeal to males   2 = Approval of males
                3 = Role reinforcement   4 = Male and female polarities

sample period. These are based on letters from the viewers. The programme followed an interview format, with a senior programme official, invariably a male, interviewed by a member of the staff who is always a female. In some programmes, the staffer referred to herself as representing the viewers.

The tone of discourse in these programmes could best be described as placatory on part of the viewers as represented by the woman, and authoritative and authoritarian on part of the medium, represented by the man. All the three programmes included questions relating to the portrayal and participation of women on television and in society. These questions covered a variety of programmes, including commercials.

A few commercials were regarded as obscene by some viewers. They wanted to know why these were broadcast when large segments of various feature films are censored by Doordarshan. The official denied that any of the commercials were obscene and pointed out that there was a committee to screen them.

In another programme, reference was made to a film which purported to examine the problem of dowry-related deaths. The viewers found that the film did not offer any solutions to the problem. While the crime itself was shown realistically and in detail, the solution offered was a fantasy. Viewers wondered whether this was because the film was an 'art film'. The explanation offered by the official was that the ending lent itself to several interpretations and viewers should choose the one that appealed to them most.

Another question related to the 'staginess' of *ghazals*, which are often accompanied with shots of birds, flowers, rivers and the like, while the singer plays the lonely hero or heroine. Viewers felt that this treatment of the *ghazals* was distracting. The official countered this by saying that such treatment added to the pleasure of viewing and was, in fact, a necessity, given the visual nature of the medium.

In yet another instance, a viewer commented on a health programme where the specialist was a woman doctor and the compere was a man. The viewer felt that had the compere been a woman, the questions asked would have been more detailed and open. The official felt this was not necessarily so.

Profile of Men and Women in TV Programmes

We tried to develop the profiles of the kind of men and women generally featured in TV programmes in terms of age, marital status, class, urban/rural background, etc. For this purpose, only four types of programmes were analysed—sectoral, enrichment, TV fiction and commercials. While these programmes differed in their length of duration, they were considered comparable in terms of their narrative structure. An analysis showed that, by and large, more men featured in TV programmes than women.

Table 16

TV Programmes by Sex Difference (per cent)

Type	Male	Female	Total
Sectoral	6.9 (69)	5.9 (59)	13.7 (137)
Enrichment	16.3 (163)	4.3 (43)	20.9 (210)
TV fiction	11.7 (117)	7.5 (75)	19.1 (192)
Commercials	21.9 (220)	24.3 (244)	46.3 (464)
	56.7 (569)	42.0 (421)	100 (1003)

Table 16 shows that while women featured in lesser proportion than men in most programmes, in commercials their proportion increased. A break-up of age groups (see Table 17) showed that while in the case of women, there was a marked preference for the younger age group, men in higher age groups were preferred, once again confirming the general trend of projecting them as authority figures.

Table 17

Age Group by Sex (per cent)

Age Groups	Male	Female
0–10	12.3 (70)	17.3 (73)
11–20	9.0 (51)	18.1 (76)
21–30	15.3 (87)	32.5 (137)
31–40	23.6 (134)	15.2 (64)
41–50	23.0 (131)	11.4 (48)
51–60	11.8 (67)	3.3 (14)
60+	5.1 (29)	2.1 (9)
	100 (569)	100 (421)

Table 18 shows that while it is more likely for the marital status of the men to be unspecified, women are apt to be shown as being married.

In terms of the class background, Table 19 clearly shows the middle class bias of the medium. Men and women who featured on TV had a distinct middle class or even an elite background. Those belonging to the working class had a small representation in the programmes.

Even in sectoral and enrichment programmes, the middle class bias is quite marked despite the professed educational objective of the medium. Comparatively higher representation of the working class people in the TV fiction programmes was due to *Nukkad*, which was an atypical serial.

A related feature was the urban or rural background of those who featured on television. Table 20 shows an overwhelming preponderance of urban-based people, highlighting the almost complete invisibility of those belonging to rural areas.

Lastly, the medium's preference for light-skinned as opposed to dark-skinned people is obvious from Table 21. This is particularly true of commercials and within commercials, with regard to women.

In terms of styles of dress, the preference was clearly for modern Indian styles, indicating thereby the urban orientation of those featuring on TV. The presence of people dressed in traditional Indian clothes in the programmes was not very prominent (see Table 22).

Table 18

Marital Status (per cent)

	Male				Female			
	Single	Married	Not specified	Total	Single	Married	Not specified	Total
Sectoral	—	—	12.1 (69)	12.1 (69)	—	—	14 (59)	14 (59)
Enrichment	—	—	28.6 (163)	28.6 (163)	—	.2 (1)	10 (42)	10.2 (43)
TV fiction	6.2 (35)	9.0 (51)	5.4 (31)	20.6 (117)	5.9 (25)	10.0 (42)	1.9 (8)	17.8 (75)
Commercials	7.2 (41)	7.7 (44)	23.7 (135)	38.7 (220)	10.9 (46)	23.3 (98)	23.8 (100)	58.0 (244)
	13.4 (76)	16.7 (95)	69.9 (398)	100 (569)	16.9 (71)	33.5 (141)	49.6 (209)	100 (421)

Table 19

Class Background (per cent)

	Male				Female			
	Working	Middle	Elite	Total	Working	Middle	Elite	Total
Sectoral	1.3 (7)	10.0 (56)	0.7 (4)	12.0 (67)	3.4 (14)	10.1 (42)	0.7 (3)	14.3 (59)
Enrichment	3.4 (47)	19.5 (109)	0.9 (5)	28.8 (161)	1.9 (8)	7.2 (30)	1.0 (4)	10.1 (42)
TV fiction	5.2 (29)	10.9 (61)	4.3 (24)	20.4 (114)	3.6 (15)	12.1 (50)	1.9 (8)	17.6 (73)
Commercials	2.3 (13)	21.1 (118)	15.5 (87)	38.9 (218)	0.7 (3)	29.5 (122)	27.8 (115)	58.0 (240)
TOTAL	17.1 (96)	61.4 (344)	21.4 (120)	100 (560)	9.7 (40)	58.9 (244)	31.4 (130)	100 (414)

Table 20

Rural/Urban Background (per cent)

	Male			Female		
	Rural	Urban	Total	Rural	Urban	Total
Sectoral	0.5	11.7	12.3	0.7	13.4	14.1
	(3)	(66)	(69)	(3)	(55)	(58)
Enrichment	1.2	27.5	28.8	0.7	9.5	10.2
	(7)	(155)	(162)	(3)	(39)	(42)
TV fiction	2.8	17.6	20.4	2.4	15.1	17.6
	(16)	(99)	(115)	(10)	(62)	(72)
Commercials	3.4	35.2	38.5	1.0	57.1	58.0
	(19)	(198)	(217)	(4)	(234)	(238)
Total	8.0	92.0	100	4.9	95.1	100
	(45)	(518)	(563)	(20)	(390)	(410)

Table 21

Skin Colour (per cent)

	Male			Female		
	Light	Dark	Total	Light	Dark	Total
Sectoral	9.6	5.6	15.2	14.5	2.9	17.4
	(43)	(25)	(68)	(49)	(10)	(59)
Enrichment	26.9	9.6	36.5	9.4	3.2	12.7
	(120)	(43)	(163)	(32)	(11)	(43)
Commercials	46.0	2.2	48.2	69.9	—	69.9
	(205)	(10)	(215)	(237)		(237)
Total	82.5	17.5	100	93.8	6.2	100
	(368)	(78)	(446)	(318)	(21)	(339)

Regarding the professions of men and women in all the four types of programmes, it was once again very clear that while in the case of women they were predominantly housewives, the occupations of men were more diversified. They were shown as doctors, chemists, teachers, professors, farmers, agricultural experts, businessmen, and so on. There was also an unquestionable preponderance of men with 'white-collar' jobs over those with 'blue-collar' jobs.

Table 22

Styles of Dress (per cent)

	Male				Female			
	Western	Indian modern	Indian traditional	Total	Western	Indian modern	Indian traditional	Total
Sectoral	—	13.5 (60)	1.6 (7)	15.1 (67)	—	14.2 (48)	2.9 (10)	17.1 (58)
Enrichment	2.0 (9)	25.9 (115)	7.7 (34)	35.6 (158)	1.8 (6)	9.1 (31)	1.5 (5)	12.4 (42)
Commercials	9.5 (42)	33.8 (150)	6.1 (27)	49.3 (219)	10.3 (35)	56.8 (193)	3.5 (12)	70.6 (240)
Total	11.5 (51)	73.2 (325)	15.3 (68)	100 (444)	12.1 (41)	80.0 (272)	7.9 (27)	100 (340)

3

Discussion

There is a continuity of perspective that informs the total output of Doordarshan with regard to male and female roles. Two main trends were visible in the treatment of women and their concerns on this medium—that of affirmation and of denial.

There was affirmation of a limited definition of womanhood as embodied by the physically and mentally house-bound woman, engrossed in the minutiae of home-making, deriving meaning for her existence and achievements from her husband and children. Together with the affirmation and entrenchment of passive, subordinate roles for women, Doordarshan programmes tended to deny viewers an insight into ongoing struggles of women to achieve personhood. Women in several parts of the country are engaged in isolated struggles for economic autonomy, political and legal rights, for a meaningful identity within marriage, and for relevant education. We got, if at all, token glimpses of such struggles, and even these were treated in a superficial manner.

The demarcation of public and private social spaces is a way of congealing the ongoing processes of affirmation and denial. The affirmed aspects of womanhood are situated and contained within the home, the most private of social spaces. The denied aspects of womanhood are largely located in public spaces which, as we shall see, are the domain of the male.

In effect, the construction of these two spaces results in the construction of femininity and masculinity, of gender. To retain the integrity of the public realm as male space, several exclusionary mechanisms are brought into force with the complicity of the inhabitants of the private realm. Our findings help to explicate the role of television in this hegemonic process, which is the maintenance of the integrity of the public and private realms.

The Public Realm

In a commercial for a soap, we see a young man working in his office. Later, through a crush of people in the elevator and on the road he goes to his club where he plays a hard game of tennis. When he returns home, he scrubs himself with the soap. Then, purified and sanitised after his interaction with the world outside, he goes to meet his wife. She is waiting in the garden, tea-table prettily set with lace and silver. She herself is young, soft, fresh, unhurried, quite untouched by the cares of the world, cushioned and contained within the home. She is enclosed, on one side by the walls of the house, on two sides by the garden, and in the front by the camera. There appears to be only one way to gain access to the garden where she sits, that used by the man. He is her protector and he alone has access to her. The active energetic male goes to the passive, waiting, and accepting woman.

In a commercial for a toothbrush, we are urged to enter a happy home contest. The house featured in the visual has large eyes, long eyelashes, and a large, painted mouth. The house is woman personified.

There can be no rigid, material distinction between the private and the public realms. In terms of activities we note that women often perform in public what are extensions of their private roles—that is, they work as child-minders, nurses, maids, and housekeepers in hotels and hostels. In terms of the locus of decision-making, we note that both in our culture and in the media it is men who make the comparatively more important decisions within the home and wield greater economic autonomy. The distinction that we sense intuitively and emotionally will have to be crystallised in ideological terms.

O'Brien (1982) notes that the Marxists offer a partial explanation about why certain men had access to the public realm by defining that realm as the social space within which the ruling class is free to perpetuate the praxis of its own survival *qua* the ruling class. She goes on to add that for feminists, focusing on production processes as the basis for the establishment of ruling class hegemony is unsatisfactory and proposes that we concentrate instead on the reproduction process. Applying the dialectical model of the evolution of human consciousness to the analysis of human reproduction, she points out that for men, physiology is fate. They do not experience birth and therefore are alienated from integration with the actual continuity of species. In Marxist terms, it is women who, through their labour, create a value, that is the child. Men's reaction to their alienation from the product is to appropriate the child, that is bestow on it paternity, which is not a natural event, but an ideology. For men, therefore, potency and virility are essentially political and ideological attributes and stem from their need to cancel out the alienation built into the reproductive process. Together with the appropriation of the child comes the need to control the sexuality of the women. These twin needs result in the differentiation of the private realm from the public realm, with men effectively in control of both.

In describing the 'dualist' man, Arendt (1958) notes that the nature of man is said to be *dual*, composed of both animality and humanity, while a woman's nature is thought of as being *single*, composed of animality alone. This philosophy, cast in concrete terms, results in the separation of public and private realms.

The private realm is the realm of man's animality; it is where woman lives, and where she is governed by necessity. The public realm, on the other hand, is where man lives as a human being. This realm is created in freedom, and represents the space where man can overcome his animal nature. The private or the domestic realm is seen by men as a work-free place, a refuge from the competing world of the market place and politics. In truth, however, it is women's unpaid labour within the home which enables men to work outside it.

The distinction between these two social spaces and their respective inhabitants has also resulted in these inhabitants being marked in psychic and social ways, which differentiates them into two genders. The social construction of gender takes place through the working of ideology, which is a system of beliefs and assumptions—unconscious, unexamined, invisible—that represents 'the imaginary relationships of individuals to their real conditions of existence' (Green and Kahn, 1985).

Ideology is also a system of practices that informs every aspect of our daily lives, and though it originates in particular cultural conditions, it authorises its beliefs and practices as 'universal' and 'natural'. In the context of gender it presents 'woman' as eternally and everywhere the same. Further, ideology as a universalising mechanism offers partial truths in the interests of false coherence; it obscures the actual conditions of peoples' existence, and can often make them act contrary to their own existence (Green and Kahn, 1985). In the last section of this discussion, when we consider the support structures for male hegemony, we will enlarge on two major Indian epics, the *Mahabharata*, and the *Ramayana*, as universalising ideological mechanisms that even today are implicated in the construction of femininity.

Cross-culturally, gender is found to be a learned quality, an assigned status, with quantities that vary independently of biology and an ideology that attributes these qualities to nature (Mackinnon, 1982). Further, when *woman* as a social construct of contemporary industrial society is analysed, the *gender* stereotype so constructed is in fact found to be a *sexual* stereotype. Thus descriptors like docile, soft, passive, nurturant, vulnerable, weak, narcissistic, childlike, incompetent, masochistic and domestic that are generally used for women, gain their validity only in apposition to 'male' activities. Socially, femaleness means femininity which means attractiveness which, in turn, means sexual availability on male terms. Thus, through gender identification, women see themselves as sexual beings that exist for men (Mackinnon, 1982).

When women enter the public realm, they continue to be governed by gender stereotypes in diverse ways. Ferguson (1982) points out that the shift from patriarchal ideology based in the male-dominated family to a more diffuse masculinist ideology has resulted in a shift in power from fathers and husbands to male professionals and bosses. Michel Foucault (1979) in tracing the history of sexuality notes that the rising bourgeois class gradually creates a new ideology for itself that shifts the emphasis from control of the social process through marriage alliance to the control of sexuality as a way of maintaining class hegemony. In public, this dynamic exhibits itself as a metaphorical father–daughter relationship, with the daughter as eternally ignorant and the father as consistently knowledgeable and discursive.

It is thus difficult to agree with Jane Gallop who complains that both psychoanalysis and feminism flounder in the familial interpretation of power relations. While psychoanalysis considers revolutionary conflict along a parent–child model, thus reassimilating larger social issues into the familial domain, feminism, with its insistence on 'men-in-power', endows men with a sort of 'unified' phallic sovereignty that characterises an absolute monarch and which bears little resemblance to the actual power in our social, economic structures. This model reproduces the daughters' view of the father (Gallop 1982).

We believe that Kakar and Ross (1986) come closer to enunciating the problem when they note that besides its roots in the unconscious wishes and desires of individual fantasy, the conception of the daughter as the sole creation and possession of the father also reflects the reality of the traditional Indian social structure. The creation myths which describe the birth of Saraswathi, the Goddess of learning, point out that she was the mind-daughter or *Manasaputri* of Lord Brahma. Saraswathi is depicted without a consort, but stories abound of Brahma's subsequent sexual consumption of her. If sexual consumption can be understood as intellectual control, this myth can help us understand the irreversible knowledge-giving–knowledge-taking interaction between men and women.

We will examine three public service commercials and two fiction narratives to elucidate this point. The first, to explain the proper use of telephones, was made for the government department of telephones, and features a number of disruptive women. To begin with, there is a young pretty girl, whose extended love-talk over a public phone causes a log-jam of busy, irritated men. The male authoritative voice admonishes, 'Keep love-talk to the minimum.' Never shown on screen is the male interlocuter, whose complicity made possible the long conversation. In the next scene, a man about to leave for work is obliged to call his female neighbour to his phone. As all women, she is loquacious and quite oblivious of the need to be brief. The busy man frets and fumes. In the third scene, two teenaged girls play a popular record over the phone; both dance for long minutes to the tune. Once again the male authoritative voice comes on to berate them.

A more serious problem is posed by another short film. Here a busy executive suffers a heart attack in his office. He tries in vain to reach his wife. She is busy gossiping about knitting patterns and parties. Finally, the man is taken to the hospital. This time, the woman secretary takes the wife to task, though the film ends with the mandatory male voice-over. It is not clear, however, why the man persisted in calling his wife. Surely calling his doctor, or clinic or the nearest hospital emergency ward would have been more feasible?

The third short film is set in a hospital intensive care unit and purports to educate viewers about the correct deportment to adopt in such places. A young woman patient suffering from a heart attack is considerately cared for by everyone, but (unbelievably) her own mother. The mother, evidently the last to know of her daughter's condition, is loud, brash, overdressed, and stupid. She declares she is too busy with her social rounds to visit her daughter during the specified visiting hours, and argues so loudly with the nurse that the patient suffers a relapse. Once again, the male voice evaluates the woman's reprehensible behaviour. Two stereotypes clash in this film—the nurturing mother with the loud-voiced, strident woman— and the negative one wins.

In one serial, a retired judge, distressed by the plight of women in his immediate vicinity, resolves to help them through voluntary service. Several episodes of this serial show the judge and his friend, a retired police commissioner, tackle issues of dowry, widowhood and so on. The judge's educated, wealthy, home-bound daughter-in-law is shown involved in a women's club, attempting to raise money to build a swimming pool. She is educated about the need to use the money to build public toilets for slum dwellers. In another episode, the daughter-in-law is seen begging her husband for a page of his newspaper to read at breakfast. Quite viciously, he informs her that the paper is not a deck of cards to be distributed, and anyway all she would be interested in is notices of garment sales and new face creams. Later the woman is shown with an egg mask on her face, and is again viciously baited by her husband. The metaphoric father's intelligence can be appreciated best if offset by the incredible stupidity of the metaphoric daughter.

The elements of sarcasm and subterranean violence that inform this narrative and the three commercials discussed earlier are missing from the serial on the lives of Indian freedom fighters. In the episode under review, the young freedom fighter notes his wife's restlessness. She expresses her loneliness and desire to be involved in his work. The husband takes her to meet his mentor. The mentor welcomes the idea and gives the woman a set of hand-spun clothes to wear. As befitting the followers of Gandhi, the symbolic father–daughter interaction is here imbued with gentle guidance. The woman's social and political initiation is in effect a rebirth, and to make this plain, the narrative shows her cutting off relations with her wealthy and unsympathetic father.

Thus in the public realm, whether through sarcastic coercion or sweet reasonableness, the preferred male–female interaction depicted is that of father–daughter.

One mechanism which ensures the continued subordination of women within the public realm, is the ideology of marriage as the ultimate goal for them. This results in women seeing themselves as temporary, part-time or emergency earners and seeking jobs that are extensions of their housekeeping roles and that capitalise on their socially acknowledged assets, their physical charm.

Television discourse confirms the 'woman as essentially home-bound' ideal in many ways. In the commercials sampled, we did not come across a single case of young professional women endorsing any product. They were either young and unmarried, in which case they were seen in situations of leisure, or they were young and married, in which case they were seen engaged in domestic tasks. In programmes for women, interviews with women employed outside the home repeatedly stressed the effect of the woman's job on the family, and applauded her felicitous handling of both. Women entrepreneurs, women judges, women police personnel were all routinely subjected to the same set of questions which focused on their husbands' responses to their jobs and the cooperation they obtained from them. The husbands were projected as exceptional, generous and unusually cooperative. The real message being projected through these programmes was that of exceptional women engaged in juggling two jobs and a subtle warning to female viewers that if they were not fortunate enough to enjoy family support, they had better remain within the ambit of the home.

Training for women was usually discussed at the 'skills' level, that is, women were prepared for jobs that would enable them to function as supplementary or emergency earners. The options emphasised jobs that were mechanical and routine and which did not necessitate profound changes in household structure. Jobs like stenography, fashion design, beauty culture are flexible and do not have to be pursued as vertical-growth careers, with provisions for promotions, increased status and earnings, old-age and medical benefits, dependent on unbroken stretches of service. Teaching and nursing are also women oriented and, together with other jobs mentioned earlier, are seen as task rather than policy-oriented.

Thus teaching, which in its essence is a deeply intellectual and, at the same time, a subversive activity, is approached by our society as a mechanical chore, ill-paid and ill-prospected, and as such jobs, usually are, reified. Because of these reasons, all the jobs promoted as being ideal for women, are transplantable, that is, they can be relocated according to the needs of the husband's career. The women's real career thus lies within the private realm.

Another set of exceptional women seen on screen were the participants in the political arena and the revolutionaries. Considering the high visibility of women in our freedom movement and their much-lauded participation in it, it may appear strange to label them 'exceptional' especially as they were held to be complementary to men. But this dynamic of complementarity lasted only as long as the movement lasted. Once the situation became stable, women were once again excluded from the public realm. Two fictional narratives reiterated this 'emergency' role of women. Mackinnon (1982) rightly notes that the concern of revolutionary leadership for ending women's confinement to traditional roles arises from the need to make their labour available to the regime. Women become as free as men to work outside the home, while men remain as free of it within. Women's labour and militancy are both coopted. Just as our freedom movement remained a partial revolution (we only exchanged one set of rulers for another without disturbing the structure of Indian society), so women's participation remained partial. They operated within narrow, male-defined limits which did not alter the structure of male–female relationships.

Agriculture, no less than politics, was presented as a public realm in which women could negotiate roles only as wives or entertainers. In programmes for farmers, women invariably appeared as entertainers, singing folk songs or dancing. The actual work was presented as purely male activity, with hard-working men turning to dancing and singing as a respite. Commercials sponsoring farmer's programmes also reflected this theme, with males discussing fertiliser inputs, tractor hire and crop prices, while the females adorned themselves. The man-as-earner and woman-as-consumer ideology was propagated even by public sector units.

Programmes about inputs to stimulate progress in agriculture also had male farmers as their target. Thus the visual of a mechanical paddy transplantor showed a man wielding the machine whereas in the field, this job is women-intensive. Women's involvement in agriculture was limited to kitchen gardens. In one programme, the camera travelled to the kitchen garden of the Vice-Chancellor of Haryana Agricultural

University. His wife was interviewed on this programme. She was asked if she popularised kitchen gardens among her friends while her husband was asked 'technical' questions relating to fertilisers, pesticides, etc. In the background could be seen labourers engaged in weeding and caring for the plants. The focus in this programme was on the women's role as home-maker, overseeing the home-based production of domestically consumed articles. The man, in command of technical expertise, was affirmed as one whose expertise was at the service of the public at large.

Although in the programme on women artists the compere was female, two males were invited as experts. One of them noted that the works featured exhibited no tension, because in the Indian society women and men had equality of opportunity and expression. This palpably absurd remark went unchallenged by the compere. One woman artist, who had changed her medium from oil to fabric collage, said that at first she felt like a housewife as she went about with her fabric and scissors. Her self-esteem and identity as artist was validated only when she went on to win awards for her work. We can now appreciate Barrette's remark that the meaning of gender in patriarchal discourse is not simply 'difference' but 'division, oppression, inequality and interiorised inferiority for women' (Barrette, 1980). With the division of social space into public and private comes the labelling of public as superior and private as inferior. When women enter into complicity with men in devaluing work within the home, they assist in the hegemonial process of valourising men's work.

The construction of the public realm as male space, as we have seen, confirms male authority. This is most evident in the news bulletins which are records of male activity. News is information about recent events. To think about news is to make important assumption about time, events, and ways of informing the people. These assumptions have their roots in socially defined reality; they reflect the way a society or culture views the world (Mckinley, 1983).

On Doordarshan the news bulletin is a highly structured programme. News relating to political, economic and developmental activities is followed by news about sports and finally, the weather. Mckinley notes that that news sequence is one which moves from events at the centre of culture, that is problems of government, business, religion and so on, to athletic competence, which is the cultural cultivation of natural abilities. Finally, concern is expressed over those aspects of nature not subject to human control, that is the weather.

Our findings about the structure of news programmes support the findings of similar researches. We noted that political news formed about 45 per cent of the content of every bulletin. The first 10 items of every bulletin also dealt with political news; 66 per cent of the time in the case of Hindi bulletins and 66.3 per cent in the case of English bulletins. Smith (1979) reported that in his sample, the government was the dominant subject, the primary actor, and the primary acted-upon. Government investigations, hearings and meetings provided the single largest category of news subjects, and governments at the city, state and federal levels were the subjects of more than half the stories in the sample.

In our sample, more than 60 per cent of the newsmakers were celebrities, more often than not political leaders of the ruling party representing the government. Of the newsmakers in our sample, 72.4 per cent were male, and 40.3 per cent of them made news in the political context. Women made news in 6.5 per cent of the cases; here, too, they were largely politicians and government functionaries. Mckinley (1983) noted that the structure of society itself provides the context for interpreting newsworthy events. Since our society is deeply androcentric and class-divided, the criteria of significance and selection of newsworthy items are determined by this framework. Thus, not only women, but the poor and the disadvantaged are also excluded. Our findings show that if women made news as individuals, they were celebrities like politicians or Wimbledon stars. In groups, they were shoppers during hours of curfew relaxation or victims of calamities. *En masse* they were featured as audiences at public rallies, passively listening to politicians. On the other hand, a report of an opposition-organised protest where women were described as participants was not supported with visuals. The collective strength of women as actors was thus rendered invisible.

Green and Kahn (1979) help us to understand the invisibilisation of women in the news when they quote Lerner (1979), who noted that as long as history (news) has as its primary focus 'the transmission and experience of power', and as long as 'war and politics are seen as more significant to the history of humankind than child rearing', women will remain marginalised or invisible.

Women and the poor featured largely in the 'deaths and disasters' and 'development news' category. Even in the case of development news, as Ignatieff (1985) has noted, the government remains the actor. The shift in focus to the disadvantaged sections of society is supposed to balance government handouts; instead, the inclusion of the so-called human interest stories, according to Ignatieff, has destroyed the coherence of the genre itself. While we do not completely agree with this, we hold that the inclusion of the human-interest stories, embedded in the matrix of political stories, is more in the nature of providing relief from the grim business of life itself. It is a devaluation of the lived experience of the poor and the marginalised of society.

The Joshi Committee Report (1985) has strongly decried the tendency of television news to be oriented towards the activities of political and other celebrities. It notes: 'The viewers of Doordarshan live well above the poverty line and Doordarshan, through its VIP-oriented news programmes and trivial entertainment, promotes complacency, and a drugged indifference to issues of social transformation, rather than any self-questioning of their life-style on the part of its middle and upper class viewers.' We agree, and feel with Ignatieff that '. . . television (news) is worshipping state power and insisting that we do so as well. It is power itself—the sacred offices of state—that is worshipped'.

Both enrichment and sectoral programmes as well as commercials celebrate men's power to evaluate the world in general and women's activities in particular. The pattern of compering followed by the enrichment and sectoral programmes illustrates this trend, as does the use of men as experts in all fields and on all occasions. Commenting on this disturbing trend, a media critic has pointed out that '. . . women lawyers, economists, women of real intellectual calibre and social conscience have been kept off the screen.' She points out that, by and large, only women sympathetic to the establishment participate in important interviews and discussion. 'One woman who was asked to participate in the *Sach ki Parchaiyan* programme on women was hastily dropped when she said she would mention Shah Bano' (Malik, 1986). The reference was to the controversial Muslim Women (Protection of Rights on Divorce) Act 1986, which most women see as a retrogressive measure. The medium thus persistently denies women's insights into what are seen as matters of public policy; their visibility is noted only at the level of tasks to be performed. Women are projected as reacting to situations, as if they never, at any point, have a dissenting voice to raise. Alternatively, they are presented as expositors, not as original thinkers. Thus, on women's programmes and health programmes, women, as doctors and citizens can be heard talking of the need to delay marriage and child birth in terms of rise in birth rates, and the need to give the woman time to develop into a 'better' wife and mother. But we get to hear very little about the effect of early pregnancies on the physical and mental development of the woman herself.

Comperes and experts on women's programmes repeatedly stressed the need for women to use clean water for drinking and cooking purposes. Women activists and development workers, and indeed citizens who have experienced the mirage of clean water at the most personal level and who can thus ask pointed questions relating to developmental priorities, are never heard on such programmes.

In commercials, as we have noted, the authoritative male voice not only endorses the product, but also the woman's competence in selecting and using it. Or else the intelligence differential is painted in bold, clear colours, as in the commercial for a toothpaste where the male voice asked if the woman's present toothpaste cared for her gums. 'Gums?,' asked the woman with an expression of utter imbecility, as if she, young, urban, English-educated elite, had never heard the word before.

When women endorse commercial products, their voices are usually seductive or caressing. Only two authoritative women featured in the sample, both endorsing detergents. When a woman endorsed a toothpaste, she referred to the age-old practice of using the oil of cloves for tooth care. The jingle emphasised grandmother's lore. But it is the male dentist who has the last authoritative word. Any product or description of a product which at all hints at technicality, necessarily has to have male endorsement.

The male as technical expert is projected in a series important to our understanding of the medium. This is the audience contact programme. *Aap aur Hum* provides a direct window to the process of programming, and in the absence of independent research, the only one. It is based on the system's response to carefully selected viewers' letters. Over the years, this selectivity has fashioned a certain kind of interaction with the viewers. Viewers who want their letters answered on this programme know what will be selected and accordingly write on those subjects. Thus their questions (programme-wise) generally relate to feature films, film-based programmes, dramas, sports, and programmes based on dance and music.

Also predictable are the kinds of questions asked. They invariably pertain to the timing of programmes, choice of comperes and interviewees, and comments on studio sets. Political programmes are never discussed, nor is the level of treatment of any programme. Of the sectoral programmes, the ones for children feature occasionally and sometimes, there is a question relating to the *Ghar Bahar* programme in the women's series. The farmers' programme has its own letter-based programme slot.

The format of the programme is a question-answer session. Reader's queries are read out by the staffer (invariably female) and are answered by a senior official of Doordarshan (invariably male). This irreversibility of roles has been widely commented upon, and the point is well taken. Our concern is somewhat deeper. On several programmes, the female staffer has said that she represents the viewers. This perspective is important, for we are well able to appreciate the powerlessness of the viewers vis-a-vis the medium.

A media critic has noted the contempt with which Doordarshan generally treats the viewers. 'Total war was declared on those who had written in. Not only did Doordarshan dismiss all dissent with contempt but viewers who had written in were just asked to lump it' (Malik, 1986). The following example aptly illustrates this supercilious attitude. When a viewer wrote in that programmes for rural women should provide information on constitutional and legal rights, the official asserted that at the moment such information would not be appreciated by the rural women as they were not ready to receive it. While the statement itself was factually incorrect as some earlier programmes had already dealt with women's legal rights, what was important was the casualness with which the question was dismissed. The immediate impulse was to defend the apparent absence of such programmes, and to transfer the onus of responsibility on to the viewers, i.e., that they were unprepared to receive it.

The incident is just one example of the dismissive casualness with which Doordarshan generally ragards the view of its viewers. On other occasions, the programme hosts have expended time on trivia and thereby skirted the really vexing questions of policy. Sometimes, the questions have been treated with light-hearted banter so as to give the impression of openness and frankness. Under the facade of obtaining feedback and eliciting audience participation, Doordarshan has in fact continued to exercise complete control over every aspect of its programming.

The tangible, visible, male–female interaction on this programme, that of male authority/superiority and female ignorance/helplessness, is evocative of the actual relationship between the medium (represented by the male) and the viewers (represented by the female). This aspect will be of considerable importance when we go on to discuss the future of women's concerns on television.

As we have noted earlier, the male need to cancel out his alienation from the actual experience of integration with the continuity of species has led to the appropriation of the child. O'Brien (1982) points out that it has also led to the construction of structures of continuity to overcome this alienation—marriage, gods, inheritable property, in fact the whole idea of the state. In these structures, both women and the working class find only token representation. In our analysis of men and women in four categories of programmes, we noted that women featured largely in commercials. Most of these women fell in the age group 21–30 years. Both men and women were generally urban-based. The working class was poorly represented in all categories (21.4 per cent males, 9.7 per cent females). These figures were due to two serials that depicted working class characters. In terms of skin colour, some 82.5 per cent males and 93.8 per cent females were distinctly light-skinned. Commercials accounted for the heaviest concentration of light-skinned females. The hegemonial pattern is thus clear: the preference of the medium is for men over women, middle class over working class, urban over rural, light-skinned over dark-skinned.

Cantor (1980), quoting the research of Glennon and Butsch into the depiction of working class life-style in television serials, notes two recurring themes—one, of the working class husband/father as a bumbling fool, and two, of the children as dignified, upwardly mobile professionals. Further, when male dominance is the norm for middle class and elite dramas, working class narratives reverse this trend. In other words, the working class man is a deviant because he is a fool and under the control of his wife.

In one television fiction narrative that focused on the working class, there were a number of comic characters—the policeman, the drunk, the hero's side-kick. Each was shown as dreaming of upward mobility. The leader was projected as being better educated, better spoken and more tolerant of the foibles of his fellow-men. His technical profession, sense of humour, absence of idiosyncratic speech differentiated him from the others. This man was a leader who had arisen from the masses, empathetic and non-exploitative. The women characters were largely dependent on the men. The one autonomous woman character, the teacher, though shown as repository of wisdom and dignity was weakly delineated. She appeared as a middle class arbitrator of working class quarrels. While the serial was about the working class, the values endorsed of individual upward mobility were those of the middle class. The inhabitants of the street corner did not organise themselves to fight the exploitative conditions under which they lived, at least in the episodes sampled. While the characters expressed awareness of their social reality, they often appeared reconciled to it.

The central character of the other fiction narrative also belonged to the working class. He was a male servant in the household of an urban, upper class businessman. Though the title song reiterated the servant's uncompromising integrity and his ability to speak his mind forcefully the man was in fact a role model for a feudal servitor, loyal to his master's household. Within the household, the relative positions of man and wife, parent and child, and man and servant were maintained and entrenched.

In one episode, the wife was held responsible for facilitating the theft of her jewellery by keeping it at home instead of in a bank's locker. In the quarrel that followed, the husband described the issue as being one of insubordination. The servant managed to make peace between them and the quarrel was forgotten. But the point was made. The woman's economic freedom was in fact severely limited and she paid the price in terms of her subordination to the master earner.

What are the effects of having significantly more prominent men than women on television? On the basis of her ongoing research into sex roles on Canadian television, Williams (1986) suggested that

—— There are fewer role models for females than males; this is especially important for children.
—— It becomes difficult to provide variety in the portrayals of prominent females, which leads to stereotyping.
—— The consistent portrayal of more men than women leads to the implicit message that females are less important than males.

She noted further that the consistency of such survey results and the apparent resistance to depicting women as important, knowledgeable and authoritative appeared to be consistent with the 'keep men in power' viewpoint of Gerbner (1978) and Tuchman (1978). With regard to Indian television, we hold that the drive is to shore up male ideology rather than males themselves. The activities of women ministers and politicians of the ruling party are also given fairly extensive coverage. As we noted in our theoretical considerations, such apparently felicitous findings can result from the mechanical application of content analysis techniques.They need to be interpreted in the light of the Indian emphasis on the government as actor.

Women are thus allowed a precarious foothold in the public realm under certain well defined conditions. Such conditions serve as exclusionary mechanisms. Thus, the prescription states:

—— Women are temporary or emergency earners/participants. They have to go back home once the emergency is over. The temporary, unmarried state is also emergency-related.

—— Their choice of jobs should be limited to spheres.which do not disrupt the household and do not challenge the importance of the male.

—— When women aspire to careers rather than jobs, they can do so only because they are supported by exceptionally large-hearted men.

—— Women are consumers, men are producers. Hard-working men can find respite either through their sheltered caring wives, or through programmes of music and dance.

—— Women understand their presence in the public realm as an intrusion into male space and express this understanding through veiling their faces, modulating their voices, and hiding their intelligence.

We need to take note of the many dissenting voices that refuse to valourise the public realm. Rogers (1978) quoted in Green and Kahn (1985) asks why research takes no note of women's involvement as matchmakers or as sharers in wealth or higher status. Further, if women are kept away from public life, are they necessarily inferior? Why should we give priority to public life, and why devalue women's importance in less formal, private roles?

We need to seriously address ourselves to this problem. While it is true that we should not use categories (such as private and public) to challenge the ideology from within which they arise, we have to note that however important women's work is within the private realm, it still places them effectively under male control. We need to challenge, as we noted earlier, the interiorisation of this control. Further, in the Indian context, women are placed under male control precisely by apportioning to them such 'important' work. If autonomy was part of women's lived experience, would we, as a nation, experience ever-rising levels of female foeticide, female infanticide and dowry-related deaths? All these phenomena require female complicity and such complicity arises only from women's interiorised inferiority.

It is pertinent to end this discussion of the public realm by noting yet another mechanism that controls women's entry into and behaviour within this realm. This is the construction of the 'woman-as-seductress' model

Women are highly visible in television discourse, particularly in commercials and art and entertainment programmes. Even as spot announcers, women perform a highly decorative function for they are usually glamourously dressed. There is an exception, however. During periods of national mourning, like the one witnessed in the early part of our sample, such programmes were absent. Programmes of light music, dance, and film song sequences, were replaced by programmes of religious music. Women participants were soberly dressed, as were women announcers. This change was marked, as there was no difference in the appearance of male performers and announcers. Thus we learnt that during periods of national mourning, when the nation's heart is wracked by loss, decorative women are unseemly and must be banished from the public realm. A popular hymn telecast during such mourning periods reflects this attitude towards women:

> Seek Govinda, seek Govinda, O silly mind
> Perceiving the ample breasts and navels of women,
> Do not succumb to impulses of passion
> These are only modified forms of mere flesh and fat
> Realise and reflect upon this in your mind, time and again
> (from *Bhaja Govindam*, a hymn by Adi Shankaracharya)

This hymn often has women members as part of the group of singers.

The Private Realm

Vegulipenn, a Tamil film made over two decades ago, was telecast during the sample period. The film centred around an innocent, not too intelligent, but sexually mature woman. She lives with her childless married sister and brother-in-law and is shown interacting with different men, who are sexually interested in her. She becomes pregnant and gives birth to a male child, but is unable to name the father. With the arrival of the baby, the woman magically achieves maturity, and from a childlike woman unable to take care of herself she is transformed into a responsible nurturing female. After many twists and turns, it is revealed that the brother-in-law is the father of the child. The elder sister now dies, happy that her most ardent wish for her sister, that she find a husband as worthy as her own, has come true.

Analysed as a fairy tale in the style of Bettelheim (1976), this narrative can be read as that of a single, unfulfilled woman, who is made whole by the arrival of the child. The 'sick' sister is the alter-ego of the healthy, mature woman, whose long but fruitless marriage has left her incomplete and unfeminine. In other words, her distancing from the world has put her into a trance-like state, comparable with that of Sleeping Beauty and Snow White. The trance is broken by the kiss, in this case sexual consummation by the Prince or the Ideal Man. This man is the loyal male, who suffers his wife's childlessness with calm strength. About the 'sleeping woman', Bettelheim says, 'The world comes alive only to the person who herself awakens to it. Only relating positively to the others (chosen life partners) 'awakens' us from the danger of sleeping our way through life. The kiss of the prince breaks the spells of narcissism and awakens a womanhood which upto then has remained undeveloped. Only if the maiden grows into a woman can life go on.' Bettelheim explains further that sexual awakening is equivalent to the birth of a higher ego and fairy tales reassure the child that traumatic events like menstrual bleeding or intercourse do have happy consequences. In some versions of the Sleeping Beauty tale, the awakening occurs only when the baby feeds at the woman's breast. This, to Bettelheim, signals female completeness, the summit of femininity.

A feminist reading of this text can point out, not the universality of the human condition implied by Bettelheim, but pervasive phallocentricism. Using the theory of suture (see, for instance, Silverman, 1983), it is possible to discern that the married sister is obliged to confess to a *lack*, a lack which is made good once her *alter ego* provides her husband with a son. In other words, the son's arrival raises her to the position of an Ideal Woman in patriarchal society, and also brings the narrative to a perfect closure. Ruth (1980) charts the course that the ideal Man and Woman have taken in the patriarchal order.

Ideal Man	*Ideal Woman*
Powerful, creative, intelligent, independent,	Nutrient, supportive, intuitive, emotional, cunning, needful,

self-reliant, strong	dependent, tender.
Courageous, daring	Timid, fragile
Responsible, resolute	Capricious, childlike
Temperate, curious, sober	Ebullient, exuberant
Honest, forthright	Tactful, evasive, artful
Self-affirming	Self-denying
Confronts world	Withdraws from world
Authoritative, decisive	Compliant, submissive

Over the course of many centuries, the ideal has been transformed into a stereotype, in the sense that these descriptors have now become 'habits of thought' with us (Seiter, 1986). Further, Seiter notes, a stereotype puts a 'picture into our heads' and encourages us to understand an individual in terms of traits which may be common to the group to which the individual belongs. But at a deeper level, what we are witnessing is not a sample processing of information alone; it is the operation of an ideology. Seiter remarks that stereotypes are our guarantee of self-respect, the fortress of our tradition, and goes on to elaborate that the use of stereotypes in daily life is 'full of hegemonic potential'.

The process whereby hegemony is established over a group, whether of women, or a race or an ethnic minority, is similar. A feature of the group is identified and a negative evaluation placed on it; the feature is then established as innate to the group, thus inverting cause and effect. For instance, a woman running a house has of necessity to jump from task to task, of cooking, mending, child-rearing, cleaning. This is interpreted as every woman's innate inability to concentrate on anything for long periods of time.

On television we note that the repetitive use of such shorthand as descriptors for women; attributes such as restlessness, talkativeness, stupidity and the like become metonymic for all womankind. Whereas the attributes invested with positive values by our society are metonymic for all male-kind.

In our theoretical considerations we noted the importance assigned by feminists to the male gaze and how this gaze is implicated in the construction of femininity. Since men interact with women primarily at the visual level, their first and often only assessment of the women is on the physical plane. Television discourse affirms the power of the coercive gaze in a multitude of ways.

On women's programmes, the accent is on the maintenance of a certain aesthetic level for women, both for her person and for the space she inhabits, that is the home. Hair care, home care, plant care and the like are popular constituents of women's programmes. On the commercial scene, we find the aesthetic norm carried to extremes. We have noted the large number of products for grooming aids in our sample. When women use products to enhance their appeal, they are rewarded by male approval. 'Her skin, her hair, her figure make Dimple the woman she is,' says the caressing male voice while the approved woman splashes in the pool with a man. The approval is predicated on the use of the soap being advertised. A little later, the model herself says huskily that she uses the soap all over her body, accomplice now to the objectification set in train by the male eye and the male voice. Both she and men have constructed a reality in which the woman is her body, her existence validated by male approval.

In contrast, a male musician who suffers from dandruff uses a dandruff shampoo because dandruff interferes with his profession. And although he does get adoring looks from the woman accompanist, his performance is validated by the applause of the larger world. He is not his scalp. In the construction of the cultural model of the Indian woman, attributes are drawn from both the East and West. Visually, the ideal woman is young, fair, slim, of medium stature and has large eyes. The Eastern standard of long, thick dark hair has been retained, while the accompanying wide hips, heavy bust and overall plumpness have given way to the Western slimness. The commercial for a turmeric soap shows the boyishly slim model in leotards performing yogic exercises. The male voice approves the slim body wrought by yoga and the clear skin wrought by the soap.

When women are constructed as visual objects, several objectives of the male hegemonial process are fulfilled. The first is the destruction of the woman's uniqueness. The second is her complicity in the occlusion of her intellect and intelligence. The third is the fracture of the woman-to-woman bond and the competition for male approval. Within the parameters of femininity so constructed, the woman's most saleable asset, and often her only one, becomes her body. In modern Indian society she can, on the basis of this asset, enter a number of professions, such as modelling, civil aviation, the hotels industry, and the film industry. Such professions are valourised and romanticised in all three categories of television programmes—sectoral, fictional, and commercials. In each industry, the degree of objectification is intense. Whenever discussions on these industries turn to the problem of sexual exploitation of women, it is normal to have participants belabour the woman's individual conduct, which must be both friendly and dignified. Mackinnon (1982) notes that objectification makes sexuality a material reality of women's lives, not just a psychological, attitudinal or ideological construct. This process destroys the mind–matter distinction. Desirability is made to appear as an inherent quality of women rather than a part of the social relations which create it. Sexual objectification thus becomes the primary process of the subjection of women.

Men use grooming products to enhance their masculine appeal, but though they attract women, they remain very much in control of the situation. This control stems from what Bresson (1977) termed the 'ejaculatory force of the eye', explicating the connection between masculinity and vision, with the controllers of the gaze being male and the object of the gaze being female. He notes further that though male ugliness can be overcome by goodness, female ugliness is the ultimate shortcoming, because the supreme virtue for a woman is beauty.

Caressing movements of the camera sweeping over women's bodies engage the male viewer as voyeur, evaluator and subject, and the female viewer as object. In a commercial for a soap, a young woman splashing about in a swimsuit is joined by a small girl. At the time the little girl comes into the frame, the camera is static. It is the girl who moves. She runs into the frame, stripping off her towel as she enters. We see that she is clad in a bikini. When she enters the water, her hip is angled across the frame and it blots out the water and woman. We observe the girl's hip filling the frame, and the smooth glide with which hip and girl enter the water. Apart from turning a part of the girl's body into a fetish, we are made to witness a displacement activity; though the focus is on the girl, we are always aware of the young woman, whose head was blotted out of the frame by the young girl. The girl slips into the pool, and thus 'merges' into the woman, drawing our attention back to her. We are offered a choice of two desirable females.

Sometimes the constructive gaze is openly revealed, but in terms that still succeed in clouding its coerciveness. A commercial for saris is made up of very short sequences, separated by freezes. A young woman draws a fold of fabric across the screen, and then freezes. The colour and design of the lower part of the fabric drain away, and are replaced by broad crayon strokes of colour. The male voice proclaims, 'And Garden creates the New Woman'. The woman who *is* her sari is thus openly held up to view; but the male act of 'creating' this woman is transferred to the sari.

In fiction programmes, the heroine is usually young and pretty, in a distinctly feminine way. A boyish girl is both visually but psychologically unfeminine, as could be seen in the case of two female characters. These girls are impatient with long hair and frilly dresses, identify strongly with boys in their peer group and have dreams and ambitions that centre on the world outside. In each story these girls are provided with 'feminine' contrasts. These feminine girls have long hair, wear pretty dresses, are not physically adventurous and are centred on the home and its networks of affection and care.

On news programmes women often appeared in purely decorative roles, helping male dignitaries to light inaugural lamps or to cut inaugural tapes, strewing flowers in the path of visiting dignitaries, holding a salver of medals at presentation ceremonies for sports people and other achievers. In panning across an audience, for instance at a seminar or a conference, the camera usually focuses on a pretty woman. In such interjections the camera is the extension of the male eye, and itself embodies the male gaze.

In the *Rhetoric of the Image*, Barthes (1977) noted that in photography, while denoted meaning was conveyed solely through mechanical means, connotation was the result of human intervention. Camera angles, focus, lighting are all expressive and transmit feelings or judgement about the subject of the message. When the camera picks out a sprinkling of women in an audience of hundreds of men, our idea of woman as the aesthetic, normally homebound object is continually reinforced.

We must, however, take note of the 'power' credited to a beautiful woman, not only in our culture, but by some feminist scholars too. Paly (1985), in her provocative essay *Object of the Game*, notes that the female figure on screen is lavished with attention—right from lighting to her placement in the frame. Because she commands the gazes of both those within the frame and the audience, she embodies a certain power and imparts the possibility of such power to the women who watch her.

In short, she becomes a 'persuasive ego-ideal for the female audience'. Paly goes on to distinguish between being an object in the political sense and being one in a mutually agreed situation, such as in 'play'. True, as she points out, men can allow themselves the pleasures of being an object only on the sly, if at all, but for women, objectification is a permanent political situation. Those same women who are lavished with attention on the screen, lose this attention as soon as the freshness of their youth has worn off and with this loss comes a concomitant loss in earning power and prestige. As Paly herself notes, if the objectification is not part of play, then all the connections between the state of the object and silence and submission come into force.

The *Natya Shastra* of Bharata distinguishes five types of male lovers, *chatur* or excellent, *uttama* or superior, *madhyama* or middling, *adhama* or inferior and *samprariddha* or too old and foolish. The inferior lover is one who shamelessly approaches a woman with steadfast love, even when she has insulted him and loves her even when he knows of her deceit. The *chatur, uttama* and *madhyama* types of lovers are invariably disgusted with female faults and are in control of the interaction. The culturally ideal romantic interaction is between a dominant male subject and beautiful, anxious and subordinate female object. The later *bhakti* cult credited the female perspective, and within the vast corpus of the Radha–Krishna stories, for instance, we find many in which Krishna sees the world through Radha's eyes. In the artistic treatment of this interaction we find the portrayal of androgynous lovers, where Radha and Krishna exchange clothes. For a man to be so steeped in his love would be to 'violate his primal sexual demarcation as a male' (Kakar and Ross, 1986). For Krishna, this demarcation crumbles when he changes from 'heroic' lover, for whom no woman is an exception, to romantic lover, for whom a single irreplaceable woman represents the joys of memory and attachment. This woman he would rather serve and adore than dominate and vanquish (Kakar and Ross 1986). A pretty tale is often told of what happens when Krishna returns to his people with Mount Govardhana balanced on his fingertip. The gathered people tremble to see the mountain rock on Krishna's fingers, but Krishna blushes for he knows that it happened because his heart leapt at the sight of Radha.

For the saints of the *bhakti* tradition, feminine orientation was a must. The male devotees adopted female posture and persona vis-a-vis the Lord. Love and union with the chosen one was totally envisioned from the woman's viewpoint. We may interpret the devotee's longing for union as a confession of a 'lack' which appears to be a distinctive trait of the female alone, and thus be wary of espousing the *bhakti* texts unreservedly. But through these texts, women's sexuality gets a 'voice' which is later totally silenced. What our culture chooses to remember through media is not this articulation but only female incompleteness. Thus even in dances and dance-dramas based on *bhakti* texts like *Gita Govinda* and *Goda Stuti*, we usually see the woman in the throes of longing and separation from her lover and not her initiative and leadership in the sexual interaction. Romantic love, as shown in fiction programmes as well as in dance-dramas, film songs and programmes of light classical music, exhibits polarities of male–female behaviour, with the men aggressive and confident and the women shy and responsive to male advances which often border on harrassment in the case of film songs. In this sub-category, the man–woman interaction is often quite explicit, a trend at variance with the prescriptions of the *Natya Shastra* where *viyoga*—separation or love in recall—rather than *sambhoga* or union was held worthy of public display. Dworkin (1981) notes that explicitness is the permitted sensibility and the aesthetics of objectified sexuality; this results in 'objectively' representing who did what to whom, a compulsive literalness, a construction of reality. The aesthetics of the imagination has given way to pornography. Apart from allegedly whetting jaded male appetites, such depiction can be used to underwrite the 'reality' of male virility (Lakshmi, 1985), which is often 'naturally' associated with violence against women.

Beeman (1981) noted that in the case of popular film music, music is one of the principal semiotic levels on which the film maker communicates with his audience. The 'sound' of film music, because it is part of the acoustic environment of society in general, helps to bridge the artificial world of the film and the real world of the film viewers. We believe that this resonance also works in the reverse, with film songs becoming a substitute language for vast sections of people.

Beeman and other commentators have also advanced a number of reasons for the popularity of the film song, one of them being that the urban industrial proletariat, distanced from both the 'high culture' of classical music and the 'folk culture' of the rural masses, sees in film music a 'mass culture' which is peculiarly their own. Through film songs, which are based on folk tunes, classical models as well as western melodies, film makers have tapped a powerful current in the people, thus making film music a cultural force in itself. Often the songs have no identity of their own—they are placed in the film because of their popular appeal. Their simple melodic lines can be remembered and reproduced without strain, and their popularity largely depends on the viewer's recall of the context in which they appeared (Beeman 1981).

We, too, must place the entire programme of film song clips in its context within television output, and note its immense appeal and the fact of its heavy sponsorship. We can then apprehend the dimensions of the construction of femininity within film songs, particularly if we recall Jayonanne's (1981) remark that the film song contains energy that the film text is incapable of articulating. We feel that these song sequences hold up to children and to teenagers the ultimate in fantasised male–female interactive behaviour. The truth of this observation can be tested on any urban street. There, reproduced time and time again, we find articulated at least one part of the dynamics of such inter-actions: the male approaches the female, with a snatch of song designed to express his awareness of her. The song usually contains a reference to her youth, figure, dress, eyes, bearing—in effect, her sexuality. The woman responds with indifference or anger, depending on the degree of provocation. Thus far, the event in the real world has paralleled that on the screen. What does not happen in real life is the final capitu-lation and acceptance of the male's advances by the female. Or does it? As Kappeler (1986) has noted, sex and sexual practices do not just exist out there, waiting to be represented. On the contrary, there exists a dialectical relationship between representational practices which construct sexuality and actual sexual practices, each informing the other. It is this aspect that causes dismay. We can see men appropriate as their own the male part of the discourse contained within the song sequence; could not the female acquiesce and implicate herself as well?

Within marriage, femininity is entirely constructed in the 'male-in-control, female-passive' paradigm. The Radha who could address Krishna as *tu chora* (you thief) gave way to the household slave for whom her *pati* (husband) was *parameshwar* (god) whose name could not be taken even in the most intimate of moments. Apart from being psychological, this control over the female partner can be seen in material terms as well. The men are generally older, can lay claim to a higher degree of education, and are engaged in higher status jobs than their lovers/wives. In most religious marriage ceremonies, the authority differential is underlined—the woman promises to love and obey her husband and/or is led around the fire by him. In some cultures, the man grasps the woman's big toe in a symbolic act of placing her feet on the right path. The right path for the woman implies that she must be an *ardhangini* (half of the same person) a *sahadharmini* (sharing the same faith) and a *jeevan sangini* (life's companion). In other words, her goals in life are to further the husband's aims and to create an environment within which these goals can be achieved.

Ruth (1980) points out that though in theory, a man and a woman when they come together form a dyad which contains all the characteristics valued by society, in reality the necessary meshing and interpenetration does not take place. Each half-person remains a half-person, except that the male half of the idealised whole person retains all the characteristics essential for independent survival in this world.

In television discourse, these ideologies resonate in practically every category of programmes sampled, particularly in fictional programmes and commercials. In fact, there are times when commercials almost appear to be extensions of fiction programmes. This assonance is very marked because there is no single instance of role reversal in either fiction or commercial, unless the text is structured to be corrective/ punitive. Invariably, such corrective/punitive texts are cast in the humourous mould. A serial decrying superstitious practices in women had a central woman character who is not only superstitious but also domineering, ruling over her mild husband and sons. Her alleged depredations into their autonomy are signalled by bursts of canned laughter. The harassed male is not only a figure of fun but also serves as a warning to men to retain complete control of the marital interaction.

This serial was sponsored by a company which manufactured fans. The accompanying commercial featured another 'comic' pair drawn from an earlier serial in which, once again, the wife was in control of the marital interaction. In the commercial, the woman's heel is viciously applied to the man's foot in order to spur him into action. He is then rewarded by her smile. The woman as the accelerating force behind the husband's momentum is a negatively loaded stereotype in our society; what is celebrated is the wife's quiet, unstinting service in achieving male-defined goals.

In commercials for medical products and health drinks, the nurturing wife and mother is a staple. Not only does she shop for the product, she also administers it. The product is invariably endorsed by the authoritative male voice. Except in one or two cases, the actual users of medical products and health drinks are all young boys or adult males. This mechanism, which simultaneously harnesses female energies into the service of men and denies self-care to women, confirms the woman in her 'self-lessness'. Green and Kahn (1985) explain this dynamic within marriage, pointing out that what is really being exchanged (in forging marital bonds among families) is not, as Levi Strauss would have it, an exchange of women themselves, but of the phallus. This, in Lacan's (1977) terms, is the symbol of male power which determines all order and meaning in our cultures. The woman, by consenting to her role as child-bearer, that is, reproducer of the phallus, takes her place in the symbolic and social order of her community. This dynamic serves to explain the high status accorded to women as 'mother of sons' in the Indian context.

An important serial during the sample period was *Buniyaad*. Set against the partition of India, the text seeks to overcome the alienation induced in the refugee population by affirming traditional family values. The central woman character, though a re-married widow, is placed in apposition to the well-born, elder daughter-in-law. Superficially, the difference between these two women appears to be the shrewish, rapacious disposition of the elder and the soft, self-effacing, placatory nature of the younger. Essentially, however, what validates the younger woman's existence and affirms her value in the family network is that she is the mother of three sons. This is what overcomes the resistance of her parents-in-law to her widowed past, her lack of wealth as well as her different religious orientation. Male alienation from integration with the actual continuity of the species, as we have noted, results in a feeling of essential inadequacy.

These factors may help to explain the ambivalent attitude of our culture towards women—unwelcome at birth, yet referred to as the Lakshmi (auspicious one) of the house; neglected in childhood, yet worshipped as the virgin incarnation of Devi; given away in marriage in order to gain merit in the next world, yet valued for the wealth she can transfer to her marital family. At issue here is the cooption and control of the reproductive process and hence of her sexuality.

Explaining the structures of kinship, Levi Strauss (1969) remarked that women are the gifts that men exchange between themselves (a central event in the Hindu marriage ritual is the 'daan' of the 'kanya' or virgin). In this exchange, it is the men who have the power to determine the value of the exchange and the meaning associated with it. Before we revert to our discussion of *Buniyaad*, let us consider yet another example from our fiction sample, the film *Agnidaah*. In this film, the young bride is first rejected and then destroyed by her kin because she lacks dowry. Simultaneously, the groom's father is negotiating another alliance for his son with his friend. The friend's daughter had eloped earlier and had had an abortion as well. In other words, she had violated several important taboos of Indian culture, a self-chosen alliance plus lack of virginity at the time of marriage. Nevertheless, the two patriarchs are able to negotiate a value for her—her unacceptable past weighed against her present wealth. The son acquieses and assists in the destruction of his wife.

Thus both in *Buniyaad* and *Agnidaah*, women's worth is negotiated in terms of male-decided standards. While in the former, a set of community needs (the need to ensure patriliny) is offset against a set of community norms (the need to bring in a virgin bride of the same religious orientation), in the latter, community norms are overset in favour of the individual family's need for money. In either case, the woman is not cherished for herself; extenuating circumstances are found for accepting what is considered another man's left-overs. According to a common Indian saying, a wife and a cooking vessel should always be carefully preserved, for they are consecrated by the touch of the owner and desecrated by the touch of others. Yet this prime consideration of purity can be overlooked in the interests of individual males.

In the fiction texts, we tried to discern the nature of the roles played by the men and women participating in various action sequences, in terms of their goals, the attributes necessary to achieve these goals and their success or failure in achieving them. In all of them we noted an affirmation of male hegemony and the harnessing of female energies to achieve male goals. The women constructed by these texts had no way of affirming their individual worth in the male structured matrix; they negotiated their positions on the basis of their age, beauty, child-bearing ability, and so on. In one narrative, we found the patriarch of the family faulted for his insistence on male children, because this resulted in a large family. This reversal from the normal valourisation of patriarchs occurred because the text was overtly propagandist. We feel that too much should not be read into this effort, because this narrative is embedded in a matrix of commercials, other fiction narratives, sectoral programmes, etc., which devalue women in various ways. Two fiction programmes, *Chote Bade* (a serial) and *Paisa aur Pyar* (a feature film) provide interesting examples of the ambivalence towards wealth and upward mobility as laudable individual goals. In *Chote Bade*, the daughter of wealthy parents falls in love with a struggling middle-class artist. Her mother is depicted as a grasping, domineering person who rejects the artist and seeks a wealthy groom for her daughter. This situation is exactly paralleled in *Paisa aur Pyar*.

Eventually the mothers in both texts are brought to a proper understanding of their mercenary attitudes by the men of the respective families assisted by assorted females. But, and this is important, the change in the women's attitudes comes about only when both sons-in-law have acquired wealth and social standing. That is, covertly, these men have succeeded in the male-defined terms of upward mobility, attaining wealth through their individual effort. Yet, in both cases, the women are faulted for not recognising the potential worth of the men and for not supplying a nurturing environment for their abilities. These strident women are severely punished for expressing patriarchal goals and seeking to further them in an unacceptable way, that is, unfeminine in its strength and visibility. Thus we see that within the private realm, no less than the public, the woman is circumscribed by cultural ideals. Women's programmes and commercials project the home as a work-free place, with the women contented and in control of it. This control is usually expressed through her role as 'thing-buyer'. Through thought, word and deed, however, the woman negotiates a precarious existence within this home. Humour in fiction programmes and commercials consistently inverts this power differential and thus inscribes it all the more.

Support Structures

The construction of femininity and masculinity on the one hand and the fabrication of a male hegemonial order on the other draw upon certain support structures for their maintenance. The most important of these is that package consisting of culture, religion and media.

Media functions both as the expression of a system of domination and as a means of reinforcing it. Media performs the critical task of classifying the world within the discourses of dominant ideologies (Baehr 1981). The ideology of gender is inscribed in the discourse, in our ways of talking and writing, and is produced and reproduced in cultural practice (Barett, 1980). When this is the case, being women does not automatically engender a feminist self-consciousness, for a woman arrives at a state of interiorised inferiority very early in life.

The serial *Chote Bade*, discussed earlier in the context of male and female goals, also serves to explicate the problem of view-point. Produced and directed by a prominent woman film maker, Sai Paranjpye, the message of the story seemed to be that individual effort will lead to success. The central character is a young male artist, and he finds acceptance in society (as represented by the parents of the wealthy girl) only after he has won a major prize and a scholarship to Paris. The structure of society is given—success means an exhibition in a prominent gallery, good reviews in mainstream newspapers and journals, and a brisk sale of paintings. Potential female buyers are shown as rich but without aesthetic sensibility: one wishes to buy paintings by the yard. This text celebrates male linear progress and female supportiveness on the one hand, and severely restrains and punishes female autonomy on the other. Such creativity is indicative not of a challenge to patriarchy but a 'sidling up to, a siblinghood of shared power' (Anne Friedberg quoted in Mayne, 1985). In our sample we noted that narratives by women and narratives centered on women both supported the male hegemonial order.

In *Agnidaah*, the film which attempted to deal with the problem of harrassment of young brides for dowry, the issue is certainly one that is presently engaging feminist thought and action. In the film, the young woman is shown as being educated and lively, but slowly she becomes a silent sufferer, keeping her natal family uninformed about her marital trials. Her younger sister and a friend suspect the true state of affairs but before they can take any action the woman is destroyed and the murder is passed off as suicide. The sister and friend are seen plotting a fantastic revenge, and with this the film ends.

The film does not engender feminist self-consciousness, for though it reflects the 'asymmetries of power, opportunity and situations in women's experience', it does not go on 'to envision alternative, non-oppressive ways of living' (Curb 1985). Moreover, the ending situates the young woman's revenge in fantasy, while she and her opponents are shown situated in reality. What this does to female spectatorship can only be judged by detailed reception studies. However, theorising on female viewership, Doane (1982) notes that women can become masochistic through overidentification or narcissistic through becoming one's own object of desire, thus 'assuming the image in the most radical way'. The powerlessness of women envisioned by *Agnidaah* can only lead to masochism.

The question of female viewership can be posed for every one of the 27 sample narratives. Of special consideration are those which are intended for children and the youth such as *Vikram aur Betal, Dada Dadi Ki Kahani, Famous Five, Kachchi Dhoop* and *Anmol Moti*.

The first two recycle old stories in the name of culture. Visually set in feudal times, princes and princesses, magicians and witches as well as wicked stepmothers play out their roles in highly structured ways. These stories offer female spectators options of both masochism and narcissism. Often the stories are imbued with subliminal sexual messages. A princess is kept prisoner by an ugly ogre. The princess recounts her captivity to the prince: 'When the ogre leaves in the morning he puts me to sleep, when he returns he awakens me, and then I am at his service.' These stories also train the young viewers into ways of looking, establishing early the dichotomy between spectacle and viewer, surveyor and surveyed. Judgement is intrinsic—women are rewarded on the basis of the surveyor's report.

Anmol Moti, made by the Children's Film Society is a classic fairy tale, containing all the elements of good–evil dualism: the good brother and the wicked brother, the search for one's self symbolised by the journey through a forest, the resolution of id–ego conflict, and so on. Women appear as the blind old grandmother and the good fairy. Girl viewers are thus offered the choice of identifying themselves either with the helpless grandmother or with the good fairy, who is a source of fantastic power and thus a component of the female self-consciousness. She parallells the Indian construct of *Shakti* incarnate, and is easy to operationalise in everyday terms.

The two narratives set in contemporary times—*Famous Five* and *Kachchi Dhoop*—are surprisingly similar in structure, though the first is an adventure series and the second focuses on the pains of growing up and thus on interpersonal relations. In both, the feminine principle is isolated and set off not only by male figures of authority/action, but also by female figures invested with male qualities. Thus George of *Famous Five* and Nandu of *Kachi Dhoop* dress alike, act alike, think alike and dream alike, and in their denial of 'femininity' and 'emotion' *are* alike. Young girls are offered a vision of the male and female as polar opposites, with males as central actors and females as supporting cast.

Literary history, notes Lerner (1979), has canonised and designated as 'great' certain texts which claim to embody 'universal human truths', but such truths only appear to be so because of their congruence with the dominant ideology. In our sample, the serials *Khazana* and *Kathasagar*, both based on short stories by famous Indian and foreign writers, were introduced every week as embodying timeless truths. Two episodes from each series formed part of the sample, and all but one were male-centred, with females playing nurturing mother and wife roles, or that of the unreliable beloved. One narrative was female-centered (*Suryast*), and we analyse it here to discern the 'timeless truth' it contained.

In this narrative, a young married woman is accused of infidelity, and asked to leave home and village by the panchayat who finds her guilty. Her protests are ignored and she has no witness to speak on her behalf. She can only swear on her innocence by her *mangalsutra* (marriage chain). This cultural artifact, which is endowed with great significance, and which all married women are asked to cherish and defend, proves useless as a witness to her innocence. The woman leaves, but is wracked with concern for her young daughter whom she leaves behind. As she walks through the forest, she meets a witch who helps her look into the future. The future is so frightening (her young daughter dies of neglect) that she, the mother, also collapses and dies. The commentary speaks of that day, which will come very soon, when innocent women will no longer have to die such meaningless deaths.

This text, together with the film *Agnidaah* discussed earlier, poses some problems for the viewers/critic, and because elements of the women's struggle for empowerment are constantly being picked up by media, we can expect many more such examples on television.

Is *Suryast* a narrative which can easily be read as a feminist text? Certainly it takes note of existing sexual imbalances in society, but does the resolution offer a non-aggressive vision for change? Or is there a failure to strike a balance between the critique and celebration of women's oppression? The conventional narrative resolutions of marriage or death makes them prescriptive as well as descriptive, and perpetuates them as the working myths of the culture (Green and Kahn 1985).

According to these authors, writers represent in fiction the rituals and symbols that make up social practice. Each time the code is invoked, reinforcement and reinscription occurs, so that literature does more than transmit ideology: it actually creates a 'mediating, moulding force in society'. In sum, the picture we obtain from *Suryast* is that it is essential for women not to act in any way that makes their fidelity suspect; women must not only be pure, they must be seen to be pure. Such a text is fashioned along the lines of an Aristotelian drama which is a patriarchal tragedy. A radical reversal in the fortunes of the central character (in this case a woman who loses husband, child, marital home) makes him or her recognise that personal responsibility which sets the tragedy in train.

Curb (1985) notes that this is a coercive system, because the central paradigm of socio-political authority is never questioned, and is assumed to be good. In *Suryast*, impeccable fidelity for the woman is the case in point, co-existing as it does with casual sexual morality for men. To this central concern as expressed by the authorial statement, has been added as a populist measure a few lines of commentary, dreaming of a different future. However, as in the case of *Agnidaah*, the alternate script remains a fantasy. Meanwhile, the text emerges as an example of prescriptive literature which, as Smith (quoted in Green and Kahn, 1985) has analysed, is coercive, a kind of sexual propaganda. Its necessity arises from the fact that in our societies it has never been possible to exclude women in the same way as it has been possible to exclude other out-groups. It therefore becomes necessary to bombard them with a literature of religious, social and biological content, explaining why they should remain in a role secondary to men.

Another example of a 'great' work of literature recycled as a serial was *Shrikant*, based on a multi-volume novel by Saratchandra Chattopadhyaya. The works of this author continue to provide inspiration for countless 'social' commercial films. The central character is a literary person, whose story, told in flashback, always shows at least one woman at his service. Rajlakshmi, a village girl who becomes a courtesan, has loved Shrikant even as a child. Her trials are glorified, and the background song praises her softness and steadfast love, while proclaiming that the woman who waits patiently for her beloved achieves wifehood without undergoing the ceremonies of marriage.

The film begins with Shrikant talking about the intense influence of several unforgettable women on him. In Rajlakshmi we witness the genesis of the golden-hearted whore. In all the so-called 'great' works of literature, we find directed at women a number of platitudes regarding their unhappy lot, and the pious wish that they be redeemed by individual, large-hearted men. But we are provided with no hint of any structural change or of women's concerted efforts to fight their societal exploitation.

Feminists films are rare on television and on mainstream cinema. This is partly due to the problem of distribution. Feminists may be seen as a 'class-fraction'—it is they who will add such material to what Bourdieu (1980) terms their 'cultural capital'. But Bourdieu also goes on to suggest that producing for different class-fractions is an ongoing process. We can thus expect a time when what is now termed 'feminist' and 'radical' will become 'orthodox' and 'approved', if the class-fraction now consuming such material grows in size. In keeping with the national/popular collective will, the media distribution system is more than willing to absorb 'women's themes', and both Marxists and feminists have remarked on this trend.

Media cooption of women's concerns has to be seriously addressed, and the new myths thus created will, in turn, have to be deciphered to lay bare the hidden face of male hegemony. As Cagan (1978) noted, images of independent, powerful, liberated women, who are assertive and ambitious, are no longer an oddity, but have become a new cultural type. How true this is, and how easily women can be seduced into complacency is exemplified in Krishnaswamy's survey of women viewers in Madras, many of whom admired the character of Ketaki in *Khaandan*, a take-off on Alexis of *Dynasty* (Krishnaswamy, 1986). Also as Janus (1972) has analysed, media under the guise of empowering women has selectively presented issues that are marginal to the struggle. Thus liberation means getting white collar jobs, achieving equality in sports, having vacations separately from husbands. In advertisements, women are shown as having more control over consumption rather than over production activities.

Baehr (1981) agrees and notes that having more women playing police, detectives, attorneys and the like actually support structures that oppress all women. Strong women are thus reconstructed as redeemers of patriarchy. Gitlin (1979) explains the process in detail, pointing out that at all times the ideological core remains unchanged and unchallenged on television. The communication system is such that it can absorb and domesticate conflicting definitions of reality and demands of society. The basic message, because of the focus on individualism and individual solutions to social problems, continues to reaffirm bourgeois liberalism. This stance is well exposed as we have seen in programmes like *Krishi Darshan* and indeed all sectoral and enrichment programmes. This ideology suffuses serials like *Buniyaad* as well, which casts into the mould of realism the reality of Partition and its traumatic aftermath. Here too, the struggles of some sections of the refugee population, and their individual success, is presented as the formula for dealing with large-scale political upheaval.

We have already noted in our discussion of the private realm the role of ideology as a universalising mechanism. Two deeply revered epics of India, the *Ramayana* and the *Mahabharata* embody such universalising mechanisms. Both celebrate male-bonding and female chastity, or the expression of female sexuality under male control. The values of these epics pervade the fabric of our society and, by extension, of media as well.

Analysing Hindi commercial cinema, Lutze (1985) notes that apart from the overtly mythological or pheno-mythological treatment of a subject, especially in the genre of Hindi films called 'mythological', myths are used in other genres, especially in the 'sociological'. The covertly mythological or crypto-mythological use need not necessarily be a conscious one; quite unconsciously, a writer can envision an upright husband like Rama, a suffering wife like Sita, a devoted brother like Lakshmana, a duty-bound father like Dasaratha, a wicked stepmother like Kaikeyi or an evil counsellor like Manthara. In even the most contemporary of commercial films, one or more of these characters can be easily recognised.

In the film *Paisa aur Pyar*, the protagonists are modern, urban dwellers. They own factories and are wealthy industrialists. The husband, who does not control the family wealth himself, is cast as the suffering patriarch, Dasarath. The wife, whose wealth is inherited is a temporary incarnation of Kaikeyi; she ill-treats her gentle, Sita-like daughter. The daughter chooses to accompany her righteous, Ram-like husband away from the house (palace) to a poor hut (forest) where they live by the toil of their own hands. The mother is not wholly wicked (not being a stepmother she cannot be); she is made arrogant by her wealth (equivalent to Kaikayi's power over her husband) and the advice of her evil secretary (Manthara as young urban male).

The universalising mechanism comes into play when all the women are made to accept the control of their husbands. The mother is made to confess her 'lack' to her husband; in this case the lack is of intelligence, humility, kindness, the flaunting of her wealth, and non-acceptance of husband's guidance (control). The daughter confesses to *her* husband her want of 'Indianness', that is, her preference for clothes other than the sari. With the sari, she dons humility, and attains a sense of service and unity of goals (that is, her husband's goals—she has none of her own). The third woman, the daughter-in-law, at first presents a problem; we have trouble 'type-casting' her. She is a poor, working woman who lives by vending fruit. She is presented to the mother as a rich, arrogant girl, with the connivance of all the family. However, she, and the poor son-in-law, really achieve integration only when they acquire wealth. The girl is adopted by extremely wealthy people, the son-in-law earns riches and fame through his artistic merit. Thus, the two outsiders, who first relate to the central family through ties of 'love', are finally integrated within it only when they achieve wealth. The three men—father, son and son-in-law—effectively gain control of the household and the wealth of the women.

Silverman (1983) suggests that the system of suture works to constantly reinterpolate the spectator into the existing discourse. Interpolation, according to Althusser, is the way a subject is 'hailed'. Elements within the discourse set up a resonance with the subject, who then responds to the hail with recognition—saying, in effect, yes, that is me, or yes, that is what I see. Such an ideological mechanism gives the subject/spectators an illusion of a stable, continuous identity and rearticulates the existing symbolic order. The spectators are unified into non-contradictory subjects. This the *Ramayana* and the *Mahabharata* do admirably. Moreover, the *Ramayana* provides the ruling class with a model of governance called Ramrajya, a concept which resonates to this day through the Indian body politic. Gandhi envisioned the ideal Indian state as a Ramrajya. That fabled state is held up as the norm, with Rama as the ideal ruler. Leaders who do not follow this ideal are corrupt or misled. Through programmes of news and fiction, through commercials and sectoral programmes and through enrichment programmes, television harks back to this enlightened being whose compassion will ensure a better deal for the subalterns. Through such epics, and narratives based on them, key concepts of Hindu practice, such as *dharma*, *karma* and *maya* are reinscribed into the cultural memory. These concepts emphasise the value of the spiritual over the material and applaud individual acts of tolerance and charity while discouraging any analysis of the existing socio-political order.

Consider the news item on the production of a particular kind of ornamental stone at a quarry. The item focused on the export potential and earnings of this industry. Several countries where the stone is sold were listed. The amount earned in foreign exchange was mentioned. Visually, there were scenes of workers at the quarry and details of the finished stone showing its beautiful graining. At one level, this item can act as a metonomy for a range of successful governmental activity, bringing in much-needed foreign exchange. At another level, it can also be metonymic for what we know already about the conditions of quarry workers—conditions of bonded labour, the absence of minimum wages, lack of control over contractors who do not provide living space, drinking water and creche facilities for workers, and near-endemic silicosis among the workers.

Problems relating to the reality of workers' lives do feature in news programmes, but in the slot reserved for 'developmental news', where the government is shown as the actor engaged in welfare activities. Thus, reality is made to subserve the needs of the dominant groups and the process is better appreciated when we recall that such developmental news was meant to off-set government 'hand-outs'.

Another example relates to awards for women entrepreneurs. Among those who excelled were garment exporters, and excellence (success) was once again judged in terms of volume of export sales, that is, amount earned in foreign exchange. The women in this field are often from the upper middle class or elite groups, whose profits in this internationally competitive field are dependent on low overheads. Since certain basic standards are required to be maintained in respect of raw materials, design, finish and packaging of the product, the area where control can be stringent is in the matter of remuneration and working conditions for the workers, the majority of whom are women (see Husain and Rao, 1985). Thus, narratives in which the elites prey upon the poor are included in the development slot. In both stories, the reality of the elite is affirmed, and that of the poor made invisible. Viewers are required to draw morals like those of risk-taking and hard work from these stories. 'Idealising reality may alienate those who reside at the margins of the normative order, but it evokes all the more emotional commitment from those whose self-interest translates easily into condensational symbols and life dramas of the status quo.'

Values of actuality and reality are added to news programmes in other ways. The most important of these is the structuring of items within the bulletin which is then read out by news readers. In the Indian context, there are no anchor persons, and in a way this enhances the notion of objective reporting unmediated by the newscaster's opinion or personality. Another way is to ensure predictability of the news bulletins. Whatever else may vary in programming, and a lot does, the news bulletins are fixed events.

Two additional devises help augment the air of reality which pervades news programmes—one is that of time, which is flashed on to the screen at the start of the national programme which begins with

Hindi News, and the other is the weather information which ends both Hindi and English news. Time and weather both being real, it follows that what is presented in the middle must also be real.

We must understand, too, that news is also to be seen in terms of what it is *not*. News is not a serial or a feature film or a commercial, all of which are make-believe. Nor is it like a sectoral or enrichment programme, in which there is room for discussion and opinions. News is to be seen as pure information.

Finally, there is the fact that both Hindi and English news bulletins form part of the national programme, which must necessarily be transmitted by all television stations in the country. The implication is that though there may be daily local variation in programming with respect to entertainment and education programmes, in the matter of news the nation is united. By this device, viewers are encouraged to think that what is presented in the news has happened to the nation and *us*. But has it indeed? In our sample we noted that on news bulletins, some 40 per cent of the items relate to political activities; in terms of ordinal positions, these items form part of the first ten items of a bulletin for about 60 per cent of the time. Also, about 60 per cent of the newsmakers are celebrities. Both Hindi and English news bulletins are signalled by dramatic music, full of urgent percussion beats, rising to a crescendo. The content, the values of actuality added to the bulletin and the introductory music, all present a picture of Indian life as consisting of moving from one dramatic political crisis to another. Who can identify with such a scenario?

Berger (1982) notes that according to the Marxist analysis of news bulletins, news appeals to the alienated, who desire to participate vicariously in the ordering of a society beyond their control. By this analysis, news programmes appeal most to people from the middle class. The working class poor are too fatalistic to be interested in news while the rich own the means of production and have other sources of information. But the middle class, overcome by its sense of power-lessness and insignificance, has a compulsive need for constant surveil-lance, a need never to be caught napping. The mechanism of realism, most deeply inscribed in programmes of news, serves to support ruling class hegemony.

'Television is a human construct and the job that it does is the result of human choice, cultural decisions and social pressures. The medium responds to the conditions within which it exists. It is by no means natural for television to represent reality in the way that it does, just as it is by no means natural for language to do so' (Fiske and Hartley 1978). In visual media, one way of representing reality is through the use of the 180° rule, which derives from the imperative that the camera denies its own existence as much as possible. Silverman (1983) analyses the implications of this rule—what is fostered is the illusion that what is shown on screen has an autonomous existence, independent of any technical or coercive interference. Thus the camera seems to be in the position of a fictional subject, whose viewpoint we share.

This gaze within fiction serves to conceal the controlling gaze outside. The spectator is on one plane conscious of the fact that only a part of what exists is being shown in the course of what is termed 'narrative', gradually unfolded to the point of closure, when the viewer is satisfied. If this operation is successful, the spectator never realises that the 'remainder' was also a construction, and delivered to her/him through the same controlling agency. So when we ask ourselves, 'What happens next?' or 'How will the story end?', we are submitting ourselves to a powerful and unknown visual authority who, as Silverman (1983) puts it, has all the attributes of the mythically potent symbolic father combining knowledge, transcendental vision and self-sufficiency with discursive power. A successful suture operation also effectively conceals from the viewing subject the passivity of that subject's position, and this necessarily denies the fact that there is any reality outside the text.

An enrichment programme which presented this 'seamless' reality in an effective way was the documentary on the Prime Minister's visit to Mizoram. The visit followed the signing of an accord by which insurgency in the state would cease, and the people would give themselves a stable government. The Prime Minister's visit was his first to the state and he was accompanied by his wife. The natural lifting of tension combined with the curiosity of the people produced large enthusiastic crowds that lined the streets and attended the public meetings. At one gathering, a choir sang 'Hallelujah, Hallelujah'. Bridging shots showing the Prime Minister driving from one meeting venue to another carried the same song on the sound-track. The effect was that of an invisible choir, constantly offering thanks for the coming of the Messiah.

It is felt that actual social conditions are best 'mirrored' in programmes of news, which are entirely predicated on reality. The individual narratives included within the bulletins achieve credibility by

—— Introducing selective documentation which supports a particular viewpoint and discourages recognition of the possibility of other viewpoints.

—— Providing fragmentary narrative outlines. The viewers know the standard format, and so fill in the outlines themselves (Bennet and Edelman, 1985).

These authors further point out that all such narratives incorporate prior belief or prejudice into the development of the story-line. Metonomy is struck in people who share common characteristics like class, race, gender, ideology; once again interpolation is at work. In effect, these narratives are 'incitements to imagination' that reflect and reinforce social divisions. Thus reality seems perfectly objective because it has been transformed into idealised empirical and moral terms.

As far as the 'reality' of women's lives is concerned, Mackinnon (1982) has described its representation and construction as parallel activities; men *create* the world from their own point of view, which then *becomes* the truth to be described. What is objectively known corresponds to the world and can be verified by pointing to it (as in science) because the world itself is controlled by the same point of view. Legitimacy is combined with force; this hegemonial process *makes* women and verifies who women *are*. Women's acceptance of their conditions of subordination does not contradict the fundamental unacceptability of that condition, if women have little choice but to become persons who freely choose women's roles. Baehr (1981) adds that the media, not being transparent, cannot reflect the real world any more than language can. As with language, so with media: there is a process of mediation involved and this mediation is vigorously denied through a set of structures and practices which produce an ideological effect on the material they organise.

A most important way of structuring media is through what feminists call the silencing of the cultural daughter. Gallop (1982), Kappeler (1986), Froula (1986) and many others indicate instances of this cultural silencing, when women's experiences are consistently discredited and the male voice authorised, the classic example being that of the 'hysterical' woman. At the dawn of psychoanalysis, Freud, who found overwhelming evidence of rape of young girls by their fathers, chose to silence these voices and to attribute the women's trauma to imagination and obsessive passion. Examples of feudal domination, that of the sexual consumption of servant girls and governesses by their male employers were similarly suppressed. Thus, socio-political reality was transformed into a disease peculiar to women and the hegemony of men was established over both gender and class. Male power and creativity are made to appear as being *a priori*; actually, they are carefully orchestrated, and built upon women's cultural silence.

Froula notes ' . . . the hysterical—cultural script dictates to males and females alike the necessity of silencing woman's speech when it threatens the father's power. This silencing insures that the cultural daughter remains a daughter, her power suppressed and muted; while the father, his power protected, makes culture and history in his own image.' She goes on to add, ' . . . woman's silence is a cultural achievement, indeed a constitutive accomplishment of male culture.' Thus what was worthy of social criticism and structural change was transformed into a matter of individual therapy. In our analysis of enrichment and sectoral programmes of fiction and commercials, we have noted the insistent emphasis on individual change directed by enlightened men.

In conversation with the women's organisation, the Calcutta Study Group, the Prime Minister noted that 'values were dropping fast to very basic and ordinary material values . . . what is really needed is the involvement of more and more women in the functioning of our society. Here we can help and motivate, but the push must come from within . . . women must be mobilised to come out of their shells, face the challenges . . . they must function as cultural, ethical centres.' Our society requires women's complicity in protecting and nurturing a culture which has silenced and invisibilised them in myriad ways.

Ideology provides people with rules of practical conduct and moral behaviour, equivalent to 'a religion understood in the secular sense of a unity of faith, between a conception of the world and a corresponding norm of conduct' (Gramsci in Simon 1982). The *Ramayana* comprises both ideology and religion. The two theoretical consciousnesses which develop in people—the explicit as provided by religion, and the implicit, which is discerned through everyday conduct—exist in tension. The tension is resolved by pointing to the explicit as the ideal. The point is, if the majority of the population transgresses against the ideal, should not the ideal be changed? Yet the existence of the ideal strengthens the grip of hegemony. The ideal provides a yardstick against which to measure deviance, and deviance can be punished.

A recurrent problem that feminists have to confront, whether in consciousness-raising sessions, or in dialogues with academics and media persons, is that of 'reality'. Men and women alike would refute allegations of misrepresentation, distortion and partial representation in the media by pointing to the world in which they exist, in which the represented reality exists—hunger exists, as does rape, wife-battering, child abuse, genocide and refugee influx. Silly women, superstitious women, women who love clothes and jewellery, women who worry about children, women who wear bikinis, women who seduce men, women who choose their tea carefully—these women all exist. Why should we agonise over their representation on screen? In other words, what we are being offered is the 'mirror-of-society' explanation.

One way of countering this view would be to compare actual social conditions as, for example, Williams (1986) does. She notes that North American television does not mirror the social changes that have occurred over the last two decades in Canada and the USA. For example, females constitute 50 per cent of the population and about half the married females are in the labour force. But on television, representation of males has remained constant at about 70 per cent between 1954 and 1980. The occupational roles of women have changed very little between 1953 and 1979. Williams quotes a number of researchers to conclude that sex-role stereotyping does not appear to have undergone any deliberate, accidental or even random changes in the years studied.

Selective representation of reality is an exercise of power and is a constituent element of the hegemonial ecology in which women and men exist. Careful analysis of media output is needed to draw attention to its insidious effects.

4

Conclusions and Recommendations

The role of television in Indian society is that of structured subordination to the primary definers (Woollacott, 1982). Being wholly state-controlled, the primary definer is the state itself. Our findings have shown that the medium's output is biased in favour of male elites. Further, masculine and feminine genders are constructed as polar opposites. We are able to endorse through our findings the five basic characteristics of television output identified by Gallagher (1981) as common to all cultures:

—— Women are under-represented in general, and occupy less central roles than men in television programmes.
—— Marriage and parenthood are considered more important to women than to men; the traditional division of labour is shown as typical in marriage.
—— Employed women are shown in traditionally female occupations, as subordinates to men, with little status or power.
—— Women on television are more passive than men.
—— Television ignores or distorts the women's movement.

Such representation, we noted, was the consequence of the development of a national popular will, aided through centuries of religious and cultural indoctrination. The television medium, now expanding to reach the whole country, has immense possibility for strengthening hegemony. In the context of the developing countries which are oriented towards a communal, outdoor culture, the institutionalisation of studio-based television is unleashing a corrosive, coercive force. The projection of a pan-Indian culture, which our findings reveal, will, as the Joshi Committee Report (1985) notes, taint communities hitherto isolated from the hedonism and consumerism of urban life.

The recent trend towards commercialisation greatly expands the hegemonial grip of the medium. On the one hand, it consistently devalues women; on the other, it holds up as desirable the values of bourgeois liberalism, individual gain and subsequent consumerism. Thus, educated, articulate persons view their own and the country's progress and development in terms of the goods and services available to the elite. Consumerism arouses desires which distort economic priorities and lure people into artificial consumption patterns. Significant, too, is our finding that in the case of fiction and some sectoral programmes, the text of the sponsoring commercial is an echo of the text of the programme itself. At the time of writing, an exceptionally pernicious example is also available of the mutual contradiction of these two texts. *Swayamsiddha*, a television serial which purports to deal with the empowerment of a divorced woman, is sponsored by the commercial for Garden Textiles. The woman in the commercial is completely objectified; other than displaying her body and the fabrics, she does nothing at all. One barely registers her face, and nothing of her personality and achievements is known. The textiles themselves are extremely luxurious. So in the current climate of commercialisation, even feminist texts cannot be telecast without sponsorship which effectively denigrates and demeans women. Since these commercials are the norm, and feminist texts are rare, it is likely that the message of the text is processed as aberrant, and that of the commercial validated.

The proliferation of the 'serial culture' is yet more cause for despondency. Tracey (1985) quotes Irene Penacchioni on the viewing of popular television in poverty-ridden, North-east Brazil, who notes that 'the genealogy of pleasure, this joy related to the telenovella, has to be sought in the occidental history of folk poetry'. Whether or not this correspondence is accurate, it is undeniable that in our context serials such as *Hum Log, Khandaan, Karamchand* and *Buniyaad* have a massive following in metropolitan areas. Doordarshan's total gross revenue from its commercial services was Rs 31.43 crores during 1984–85; of this, sponsorship of the serial *Hum Log* accounted for

Rs 363.63 lakhs (information given by the Information and Broad-casting Minister to the Rajya Sabha).

The coercive values we have discerned within programmes of tele-vision fiction, appear to be presented to viewers through the genealogy of pleasure associated with the 'narrative' or 'story'. In this context, we have to take note of the numbing boredom generated by most of Doordarshan's in-house programmes, particularly those in the non-fiction category. Though boredom is essentially a subjective response, certain factors pre-dispose programmes to turgidity. Thus, heavy dependency on government functionaries for expert comments, near-total emphasis on studio-based programmes, unimaginative choice of comperes and participants, static camera-work, near-total absence of visuals and, worst of all, unwillingness to give time and space to divergent points of views, can all add up to very boring programmes indeed. The most hackneyed feature film or serial can attract more viewers than non-fiction programmes, a trend which helps to inscribe values which are far from empowering to women.

We have also discerned a continuity of perspective informing tele-vision output both horizontally (across all categories) and longitudinally (across time). Caplan (1985) suggests that India is ideologically highly developed, and the sophistication of its ideological apparatus goes a long way towards explaining why its gross socio-economic inequalities continue to persist. She notes that welfare schemes secure hegemony because the state is viewed as beneficent. Thus a large part of the impact of the welfare state is ideological. Through news, enrichment and sectoral programmes, the medium consistently projects India as a welfare state, with the government as the lead player, benevolently in command of every situation.

In our sample, we noted another disturbing trend: the side-stepping of local governments and bureaucracies in favour of one individual. Development is therefore presented as taking place not as a planned, ongoing, long-term process, but in order to please one enlightened, compassionate being. The basic needs of the people are fulfilled through administrative fiat, a process which subverts democratic structures. The people obtain what is justly theirs only through the intervention of the highest in the land. This throwback to feudalism not only concentrates power in one individual, but generates further dependency in the people, and cripples their ability to fight injustice. By selectively focusing on such interactions, television discourse validates and affirms this trend.

Such a trend bodes nothing but ill for women, who are struggling both as women and as the poor. Are 'alternate' media the only alternative? While the outreach of such forms as feminist journals, street theatre groups, activist groups is limited, these media play an important role in awareness-raising. They assist in the process of arriving at a different decoding of the message. Eco (1972) notes how crucial this activity is, pointing out that it is not indispensable to change a given message; it would be enough, if not better, to change the attitude of the audience so as to induce a different decoding of the message. This is the first step in the process of denying consent to the hegemonial order. Without consent and complicity, the order can only collapse. However important the movement media is, the struggle to alter the face of the mainstream media is equally important for three reasons.

First, since most of them are state-owned, the citizens, whether women or the poor, have a right to equitable representation on these media. Secondly, the relentlessly negative representation has the effect of validating women's inferiority as real and natural. Under such conditions, the messages of the movement media are likely to be decoded as aberrant.

Our third concern is with the processes by which children acquire sex-appropriate behaviour. In our theoretical considerations we have noted one process as explicated by the gender-schema theory. If children are to acquire a balanced conception of both genders, they need to be exposed to equitable representation as the norm. Stray feminist films are likely to be processed as aberrations. Hence, on a medium which is insidiously influencing tomorrow's policy makers, the requirement is for *every* programme to consider issues of gender and class equity.

This brings us to a problem which is difficult to address in its entirety—what are women's concerns? Theoretically, this is a grey area. Are women's concerns different from those of humanity at large? If we consider women's concerns as a part of human concerns in general, will we not assist in the historical process of invisibilising or 'ex-nominating' such concerns? On the other hand, if we differentiate women's concerns as separate from those of humanity in general, would we be validating biological determinism on the one hand and, on the other, severing women from those networks of care and concern in which they are situated and from which they draw psychic sustenance? To do so would be a strategic error for, as Gramsci notes, we need continuity with the past; existing ideologies can only be transformed, not abandoned entirely or legislated away (Simon, 1982).

We have noted, in the context of the construction of feminist self-consciousness, that women communicators do not necessarily succeed in breaking away from the stranglehold of patriarchy. Thus, the demand for associating more women at every level of policy-making and programming will bear fruit only if these women are themselves enabled to develop and exercise a more equitable gender consciousness. Only the development of such consciousness can enable these women to ask crucial questions about the country's development, instead of working to integrate women into the existing socio-political paradigm. Such activity will assist in infusing a feminist consciousness into all areas of human endeavour.

Harold Lasswell has described political behaviour as the displacement of personal problems into public objects (Mackinnon, 1982). Women's distinctive experience as women occurs, as we have seen, largely in the private realm. Hence there is need to demystify the sanctity of this realm. Women's programmes assist in the depoliticisation of the inhabitants of the private realm. In terms of content and adequacy of treatment, television programmes are ahistorical and succeed in representing woman as a construct that is everywhere and eternally the same.

The representation of heroic women, whether they be the Rani of Jhansi or the Supermum, does nothing to counter this trend, for we have noted that such women are usually structured as redeemers of the patriarchy. Instead, the medium should present women as comperes and experts in all categories of programmes, as well as focus on the struggles of women in diverse fields. The infantilism that pervades most women's programmes, where 'easy' ways are found to tackle 'everyday' problems should be eschewed in favour of mature, incisive analyses of social problems. Many feminists, such as Phyllis Mack (1986), suggest that 'feminine' domestic habits of thought and activity may be transposed into the public sphere and transformed into highly effective forms of activism by both women and men. Based on her study of Francis of Assissi and Gandhi, Mack further speculates that these feminine modes of behaviour gained moral and political credibility for Francis and Gandhi *because* they were being used creatively by men.

Thus the rigid strait-jacketing of the public and private realms respectively, coupled with the projection of a handful of heroic women, subverts the women's struggle for empowerment. Equality can obtain only from the integration of women on equal terms in the productive realm and the integration of men into the active care of the next generation (O'Brien 1982).

While we endorse the need to build in the women's perspective into every programme, we feel that a special women's programme has its own merits, provided that its contents reflect the larger concerns of women's experience. In our sample period, we noted the disjunction between national and global concerns such as communal and ethnic clashes, and what was presented as women's special interests—hair care and recipes for leftover bread.

However useful the local women's programmes can be, we feel the necessity to have a special programme for women on the national network. Such a programme can do much to engender in women a feeling of community.

Some years ago, the Press Council of India developed guidelines for reporting incidents of communal tension. This was done in order to strike a balance between the citizen's right to information and the responsibility of the press to contain communal conflagration. We submit that there is great necessity now to treat women as a community and to develop guidelines for their representation in media, so that media's complicity in the facilitation of gender tension can be contained.

What, then, can we recommend as steps to secure a more equitable representation for women on television?

First, we would like to add our voice to the many concerned groups and individuals who urge de-commercialisation of the medium.

Second, we suggest that concerned women's groups, in universities, voluntary agencies and government departments, establish regular monitoring groups to decode television messages. Such an activity will make education for women's equality envisaged in the education policy more feasible.

Third, we recommend that in view of television's role in influencing and shaping values and attitudes, particularly of children, Doordarshan ensures that every programme considers the issue of gender and class equality.

Fourth, we urge that communications researchers engage in methodological explorations in this area, and refine research tools.

Epilogue*

Much has occurred on the Indian political scene since 1986, when the study discussed in the main part of this book was completed. The country has moved closer to the general elections to the Parliament, which at the time of writing are scheduled for the third week of November 1989. Since 1988, the behemoth of the State propaganda machinery has been rolling with ever-increasing momentum, again on the twin tracks of affirmation and denial: affirmation of the validity of the government in power and denial of its various culpabilities.

These imperatives have seen changes both in infrastructural capability and in administrative control of the medium. Currently, there are about 430 TV transmitters functioning in the country, which reach an estimated 75 per cent of the population.

There has also been a tightening of the ideological hold on the medium: the comparative openness to dissenting voices is today overridden by coercive propaganda. Time and again the administration has claimed that extensive if not equal coverage is given to the activities and views of opposition parties. In July 1989, the Minister of Information and Broadcasting denied that the ruling party was misusing television and radio for party political purposes. In major national English news bulletins, he said, All India Radio had in the previous six months devoted 4,292 lines to the opposition parties and

* This epilogue is based on the research conducted for the Project 'Ideology of Motherhood' sponsored by the Research Centre for Women's Studies of the SNDT University, Bombay. The completed paper will appear as a contribution to the book published by the Research Centre. I acknowledge with gratitude the intellectual and fiscal support provided by the Centre and by some individual members of the research team.

Prabha Krishnan.

only 3,124 lines of news to the ruling party. For Doordarshan, the comparative figures were—450 news items stretching over 414 minutes for the opposition parties, while the ruling party netted 319 news items of the total duration of 316 minutes. A sampling of such coverage supports the point made earlier in the study, of the inefficacy of content analysis as an analytical tool. It is not only the quantity of the coverage that is important, but the quality as well. In general, the opposition parties are portrayed as lacking in ideology, cohesion and spirit of genuine service to the nation, if not as covertly subversive.

The press, which is not under direct state control, has had to fight in order to retain comparative freedom. The Defamation Bill sought to be introduced in mid-1988, succeeded in uniting the press and political activists of the entire country. The outcome of the struggle was an unconditional withdrawal of the Bill by the government. But the press and the intelligentsia were not lulled into complacency and events proved them right. The JK Special Powers (Press) Bill, 1989, brought into force in the State of Jammu and Kashmir, was seen as draconian in its outreach. Under the guise of controlling terrorism in the State, this Act eroded the right of the press and political activists to question the actions of the government. This Bill was also withdrawn due to public pressure.

In this period the country also witnessed the congealing of communal ideology. Communalism, which is used to oppose secularism, can be defined as 'the belief that because a group of people follow a particular religion, they have as a result common social, political and economic interests'. This view ignores class stratification as an integral facet of social organisation. As an ideology, communalism is ever-vulnerable to the manipulations of party politics. Increasingly, India's plural society is being reduced to majority–minority confrontation, which manouevers religious minorities into defensive positions. The irony is that the Hindu majority also sees itself beleagured on account of the educational and employment reservations as well as the special economic deals available to the minority communities. A struggle for scarce economic resources is thus expressed in terms of religious strife.

The Hindus' perception of themselves as weak and ineffectual and of the 'others' as aggressive, virile and lusting for power, adds a further dimension to the majority–minority debate. Thus organisations like the Rashtra Swayamsevak Sangh stress hierarchy and military traditions. Speeches made by those appealing to communalist tendencies repeatedly emphasise the alleged violation of mothers and sisters by adherents of opposing religions. The presence or absence of male virility and the defence of female vulnerability coalesce into an identity formation which links masculine–feminine with religious attributes. Women become symbols of culture and tradition, and need to be 'protected' with ever-increasing force and vigour.

The telecast of serials based on the *Ramayana* and *Mahabharata* during this period should be evaluated in the light of the prevailing political situation. Both the *Ramayana* and *Mahabharata* are referred to as epics of India with the first described as *kavya* or poetry and the second as *itihasa* or history. Both epics are records of patriarchal valour, in which women feature as the property of individual men. Their worth is judged in terms of the military alliances they can help forge by uniting their natal and matrimonial families, and the sons they can produce to maintain the lineage. We have already, elsewhere in this study, referred to the pervasive and persistent shadow cast by these myths on the creative consciousness of the people of India.

That these serials command a massive following is borne out by many viewership surveys. The Marketing and Research Group (MARG) conducted a poll for the *Sunday Observer*, indicating the viewership for the serial based on the *Ramayana* (Table 23).

Table 23

Viewership of the Ramayana

	Bombay	Delhi	Calcutta	Madras
Total respondents	255	217	251	238
Per cent who watch the serial	92	93	86	92
Among men	95	89	85	87
Among women	89	96	92	98

The Indian Market Research Bureau (IMRB) ranked ten serials in terms of Television Rating Points (TRPs), each point representing 1.064 lakh adults. The results indicated that the *Mahabharata* topped with 83 points, the *Ramayana* following close on its heels with 77 points. Another survey of child viewers by the Pathfinders group recorded similar findings. Of the 4463 children polled, 81 per cent ranked *Mahabharata* as their most favoured programme, with the *Ramayana* placed second by 42 per cent. An indirect way of guaging viewership is by estimating the revenue generated by advertisements. While Doordarshan earned Rs 77 lakhs in 1976–77, ten years later in

1987, that figure stood at Rs 185 crores, which is about a third of the total estimated expenditure on advertisement in the country, that is Rs 600 crores. In 1987–88, the gross revenue earned from spot advertising and sponsored programmes was Rs 136.29 crores (the average monthly revenue was Rs 11.4 crores). In 1988–89 the earnings stood at Rs 161.3 crores. In July 1989 it was reported that the gross revenue generated by the *Mahabharata* was Rs 23.60 crores, with each episode netting around Rs 60.5 lakhs.

The impact of these serials on female and male spectatorship can best be theorised if it is recalled that both the *Ramayana* and the *Mahabharata* are regarded as *dharma shastras*, that is, sources of tradition and guides to right conduct. Unlike Christian and Jewish traditions or, for that matter, Sikhism, the Hindus have no central sacred book. The sacralisation of the *Ramayana* and *Mahabharata* (which contains a late accretion, the *Bhagavata Gita* delineating the theory of karma and rebirth) was an attempt to withstand political pressures in medieval times.

We have noted that women are constructed as symbols of culture and tradition. When their struggles question the basis of male authority, religious fundamentalism provides a readymade ideology for their control. Though a number of women like Kunti, Gandhari, Draupadi, Ganga, Kaikeyee and Sita play important roles in these epics, it is Sita and that, too, the Sita of Tulsidas' vision rather than that of Valmiki's who is upheld as the ideal woman. Valmiki's Sita had her moments of authority and autonomy, but not Tulsidas'. And it is the Tulsidas version which is the bedrock for the television serial, not, as the credits state, Valmiki's version. Kunti as the mother of the five Pandawas and Draupadi as their wife-in-common are usually regarded as questioning patriarchy, rather than as being redeemers and providers of nurturant criticism. Neither is an actor in her own right.

Kunti was obliged to disown her first-born son Karna, because he was born before her marriage to King Pandu, though subsequently she had three other children who were also not her husband's offsprings. Draupadi, the *divya-janmi* or five-sprung, was the daughter of one king, the daughter-in-law of another, and a wife to five famed warriors, yet she could not prevent her humiliation in the court of the Kauravas. Throughout she is pictured as accepting her subordinate status. Her appeals for the preservation of her modesty are based not on her humanity or even her femininity; they are based on her relationships to various men, and her status as the daughter-in-law of the house of Hastinapur. Dragged into the Kaurava court while still in her menstrual period, Draupadi describes herself as being too unclean to even salute her elders. She bewails the fact that her person, which had not been exposed even to the gaze of the sun or to the touch of the breeze, was thus revealed in the company of men.

In the period of their exile, both Kunti and Draupadi constantly goad the Pandavas to action, that is, to seek revenge through war against the Kauravas. Both women reiterate and revive the Kshatriya code of honour for their men, which includes protection of their women and extension of their territories. Molested by Prince Duryodhana's brother-in-law, Draupadi cautions him to beware of her husbands—she describes herself as Bhima's mace, Arjuna's Gandhiva bow, and as the swords of Nakula and Sahadeva. Like Sita, she is sexually vulnerable and is constructed as a function of both her father's and her husband's honours.

The contrast between Draupadi and Sita can therefore be located not in the *context* of Draupadi's message but in its *presentation*. While Sita is meek, soft-spoken, with downcast eyes and faltering feet, Draupadi has a strong voice and is quick of gait, with eyes that are not afraid to look directly. Draupadi's fiery speeches questioning Yudhishtira's right to stake her person in the game of dice, after he had lost himself, and Sita's speech decrying the constant trials of purification she has to undergo notwithstanding, these women were not permitted to live by their rights: Draupadi was the first to fall by the wayside on the road to heaven, condemned by husband Yudhishtira for not having loved all her five husbands equally, while Sita had to abandon her children and disappear into the earth. There is no doubt that both women were engaged in what feminists describe as 'nurturant criticism', which serves to inscribe the male–female autonomy differential all the more, while denying any critique of the existing social paradigm.

Personal observation suggests that the viewership of these programmes is not confined to followers of Hinduism. A Madras-based Muslim entrepreneur is engaged in sub-titling the *Ramayana* in English, describing this task as a labour of love and an act of faith. A Muslim professor of a prestigious university commented that the story embodied some universal values, and that his family, including his two young sons, were regular viewers. A neighbour, travelling one Sunday morning to Najibabad in Uttar Pradesh, found her train compartment full of Muslim women regretting that their travel had caused them to miss that week's telecast of the *Mahabharata*. While awaiting detailed spectatorship studies, we can theorise that these programmes 'speak' to a vast audience. For some who are participants in the interpolation process, the serials provide a detailed portrait of 'Hindutva' or pristine Hindu culture. For others for whom these myths do not form part of their cultural inheritance, these programmes appear to provide instances of ideal individuals—ideal sons, husbands, fathers, rulers, daughters, wives and mothers.

We are witnessing a confluence of political expediency, religious fundamentalism and cultural confusion, in which the stated national ideals of secularism and gender justice are threatened with subversion. Our only hope lies in the ability of the people to 'fracture' the hegemonial process, that is, to deny 'consent' to the process of marginalisation of women and the disprivileged. True secularism cannot approve of, or remain neutral to, the content of all religions; it would have to provide a constant critique of them in the attempt to humanise them all. Where real secularism exists, programmes such as the *Ramayana* and *Mahabharata* would be an impossibility on a state-owned medium.

References

ARENDT, HANNAH (1958): *The Human Condition*, Chicago, University of Chicago Press.

AGARWAL, S.C. (1979): *Report of Sample Survey on Morning Transmission and Ghar Parivar*, Delhi, Audience Research Unit, Doordarshan Kendra.

ALTHUSSER, LOUIS (1969): *For Marx*, translated by Ben Brewster, New York, Pantheon Books.

BAEHR, HELEN (1980): 'The "Liberated" Woman in Television Drama,' *Women's Studies International Quarterly*, 3(1): 29–39.

——— (1981): 'The Impact of Feminism on Media—Just Another Commercial Break?' In Dale Spender (ed.), *Men's Studies Modified: The Impact of Feminism on the Academic Discipline*, Oxford, Pergamon.

BARETT, MICHELE (1980): *Women's Oppression Today: Problems in Marxist Feminist Analysis*, London, Villiers Publications.

BARTHES, ROLAND (1977): *Image–Music–Text*, London, Fontana.

BEEMAN, WILLIAM O. (1981): 'The Use of Music in Popular Film: East and West,' *India International Centre Quarterly*, 8(1): 77–87.

BEM, SANDRA LIPSITZ (1983): 'Gender Schema Theory and its Implications for Child Development: Raising Gender Aschematic Children in a Gender Schematic Society,' *Signs*, 8(4): 598–616.

BERGER, ARTHUR A. (1982): *Media Analysis Techniques*, Beverly Hills, Sage Publications.

BERGER, JOHN (1972): *Ways of Seeing*, London, Penguin Books.

BETTELHEIM, BRUNO (1976): *The Uses of Enchantment: The Meaning and Importance of Fairy Tales*, New York, Alfred A. Knopf.

BOURDIEU, PIERRE (1980): 'The Aristocracy of Culture and other essays' quoted in Tuchman, Gaye (1983): 'Consciousness Industries and the Production of Culture,' *Journal of Communication*, 33(3): 26–38.

BRESSON, ROBERT (1977): *Notes on Cinematography*, New York, Urizen Books.

CAGAN, ELIZABETH (1978): 'The Selling of the Women's Movement,' *Social Policy*, 8: 4–12.

CANTOR, MURIEL G. (1980): *Prime Time Television: Content and Control*, Beverly Hills, Sage Publications.

CAPLAN, PATRICIA (1985): *Class and Gender in India: Women and their Organisations in a South Indian City*, London, Tavistock.

CEULEMANS, MIEKE and FAUCONNIER, GUIDO (1979): *Mass Media: The Image, Role and Social Conditions of Women—A Collection and Analysis of Research Materials*, Paris, UNESCO.

CHANDIRAM, JAI and AGRAWAL, BINOD (1982): 'Towards Equality: Women in Indian Television,' *Media Asia*, June: 161–64.

CHANDRA, BIPAN (1984): *Communalism in Modern India*, Delhi, Vikas.

CHHACHHI, AMRITA (1989): 'The State, Religious Fundamentalism and Women: Trends in South Asia,' *Economic and Political Weekly*, 18 March: 567–78.

COMMUNICATION IN THE SERVICE OF WOMEN (1985): *A Report on Action and Research Programme: 1980–1985*, London, The City University.

CURB, ROSEMARY K. (1985): 'Re/Cognition, Re/Presentation, Re/Creation in Woman Conscious Drama: The Seer, the Scene, the Obscene,' *Theatre Journal*, 37(3): 302–316.

DATA INDIA (1989): 3–9 July: 314–15.

DOANE, MARY ANN (1982): 'Film and the Masquerade: Theorising the Female Spectator,' *Screen*, 23(3–4): 15–19.

DWORKIN, ANDREA (1981): *Pornography: Men Possessing Women*, New York, G.P. Putnam's Sons.

ECO, UMBERTO (1972): 'Towards a Semiotic Inquiry into the TV Message,' *WPCS*, 3: 103–21.

FERGUSON, ANN (1982): 'On "Compulsory Hetero Sexuality and Lesbian Experience": Defining the Issues.' In Keohane, Rosaldo and Gelphi, *Feminist Theory: A Critique of Ideology*, Sussex, Harvester Press.

FISKE, JOHN and HARTLEY, JOHN (1978): *Reading Television*, London, Methuen.

FOUCAULT, MICHEL (1979): *The History of Sexuality*, London, Allen Lane.

FROULA, CHRISTINE (1986): 'The Daughter's Seduction: Sexual Violence and Literary History,' *Signs*, 11(4): 621–44.

GALLAGHER, MARGARET (1981): *Unequal Opportunities: The Case of Women and the Media*, Paris, UNESCO.

——— (1983): *The Portrayal and Participation of Women in the Media*, Paris, UNESCO.

GALLOP, JANE (1982): *Feminism and Psychoanalysis: The Daughter's Seduction*, London, Macmillan.

GERBNER, GEORGE (1978): 'The Dynamics of Cultural Resistance.' In G. Tuchman, A.K. Daniels and J. Benet (eds.), *Hearth and Home*, New York, Oxford University Press.

GITLIN, TODD (1979): 'Prime-time Ideology: Hegemonic Process in Television Entertainment,' *Social Problems*, 26 (February): 251–266.

GLEDHILL, CHRISTINE (1978): 'Recent Developments in Feminist Criticism,' *Quarterly Review of Film Studies'*, 3(4): 457–493.

GREEN, GAYLE and KAHN, COPPELIA (1985): *Making a Difference: Feminist Literary Criticism*, London, Methuen.

GUPTA, J.P. (1980): *Women, Life and TV as a Medium for Development: An Impact Study*, Lucknow, Audience Research Unit, Doordarshan Kendra.

HARDING, SANDRA (1986): 'The Instability of the Analytical Categories of Feminist Theories,' *Signs*, 11(4): 645–664.

THE HINDUSTAN TIMES (1988): 28 January.

HUSAIN, SAHBA and RAO, RUKMINI (1985): *Invisible Hands: Women and Home-based Production in Garment Export Industry in Delhi*, Paper presented at the Asian Regional Conference on Women and the Household, New Delhi.

IGNATIEFF, MICHAEL (1985): 'Is Nothing Sacred? The Ethics of Television,' *Daedalus*, Fall: 57–78.

IMRB (1989): Quoted in *A & M*, September: 21.

JANUS, NOREEN (1977): 'Research on Sex Roles in the Mass Media: Towards a Critical Approach,' *Insurgent Sociologist*, 7 (Summer): 19–32.

JAYOMANNE, LALLEEN (1981): *The Production of Femininity in Sri Lankan Cinema, 1947–1979*. Paper presented at Women in Asia Workshop, University of New South Wales, Sydney.

JOSHI, S.R. (1986): *Participation of Women in Higher Decision-Making Levels of Doordarshan, the Television Authority of India*, Paper presented at the Conference of the International Association for Mass Communication Research, New Delhi.

KAKAR, SUDHIR and JOHN ROSS (1986): *Tales of Love, Sex and Danger*, New York, Alfred Knopf.

KANE, P.V. (1929): *History of the Dharmashastra: Ancient and Medieval Religious and Civil Law*, Poona, Bhandarkar Oriental Research Institute.

KAPPELER, SUSANNE (1986): *The Pornography of Representation*, Cambridge (UK), Polity Press.

KEOHANE, NANNERLO, MICHELLE Z. ROSALDO and BARBARA C. GELPHI (1982): *Feminist Theory: A Critique of Ideology*, Sussex, Harvester Press.

KOTHARI, RAJNI (1989): 'Cultural Context of Communalism in India,' *Economic and Political Weekly*, 14 July: 81–85.

KRISHNASWAMY, CHITRA (1986): *Indian Women and Television: A Study on the Women Viewers of Madras*, Paper presented at the International Television Studies Conference, London.

LACAN, JACQUES (1977): *Ecrits: A Selection*, London, Tavistock, quoted in Green and Kahn (1985).

LAKSHMI, C.S. (1985): 'The Vulgar Virgins of Tamil Cinema,' *The Sunday Observer*, 9, 14 November: 3.

LERNER, GERDA (1979): *The Majority Finds its Past: Placing Women in History*, quoted in Green and Kahn (1985).

LEVI STRAUSS, CLAUDE (1969): *The Elementary Structures of Kinship*, Boston, Beacon Press.

LUTZE, LOTHAR (1985): 'From Bharata to Bombay: Change in Continuity in Hindi Film Aesthetics.' In Beatrix Pfleiderer and Lothar Lutze (eds.), *The Hindi Film: Agent and Re-Agent of Cultural Change*, Delhi, Manohar Publication.

MACK, PHYLLIS (1986): 'Feminine Behaviour and Radical Action: Franciscans, Quakers and the Followers of Gandhi,' *Signs*, 11(3): 457–477.

MACKINNON, CATHERINE (1982): 'Feminism, Marxism, Method and the State: An Agenda for Theory,' in Keohane, Rosaldo and Gelphi, *Feminist Theory: A Critique of Ideology* (1982).

MALIK, AMITA (1986): 'We were not Amused,' *Express Magazine*, 13 April.

MARG POLL (1988): Quoted in *Sunday Observer*, 31 July.

MAYNE, JUDITH (1985): 'Feminist Film Theory and Criticism,' *Signs*, 11(1): 81–100.

MCKINLEY, ROBERT (1983): 'Culture Meets Nature on the Six O'Clock News: American Cosmology,' *Journal of Popular Culture*, 17(3): 109–114.

MEIER, UTA (1986): *Masculinity and Femininity in Television Drama*, Paper presented at the Conference of the International Association for Mass Communication Research, New Delhi.

MILIBAND, RALPH (1973): *The State in Capitalist Society*, London, Quartet.

NAURIYA, ARUN (1989): 'Relationship between State and Religion: Antinomies of Passive Secularism,' *Economic and Political Weekly*, 25 February: 405–6.

O'BRIEN, MARY (1982) 'Feminist Theory and Dialectical Logic,' In Keohane, Rosaldo and Gelphi, *Feminist Theory: A Critique of Ideology* (1982).

PALY, MARCIA (1985): 'The Object of the Game,' *Film Comment*, June: 68–78.

PATHFINDERS' SURVEY OF CHILD VIEWERSHIP (1989): Quoted in *A & M*, July: 44–9.

RANBIR KAUR (1970): *Impact of Television on Farm Women*, New Delhi, Indian Agricultural Research Institute (unpublished).

RUTH, SHEILA (1980): *Issues in Feminism: A First Course in Women's Studies*, Boston, Houghton-Mifflin.

SAHA, K.D. (1979): *Report on the Survey of Ghare Baire*, Calcutta, Audience Research Unit, Doordarshan Kendra.

SANKHALIA, S.D. (1973): *Ramayana: Myth or Reality?*, New Delhi, People's Publishing House.

SAYERS, J. (1982): *Biological Politics*, London, Tavistock.

SEITER, ELLEN (1986): 'Stereotypes and the Media: A Re-evaluation,' *Journal of Communication*, 36 (Spring): 14–26.

SIGNIORELLI, NANCY (1986): *Role Portrayal and Stereotyping on Television*, London, Greenwood Press.

SILVERMAN, KAJA (1983): *The Subject of Semiotics*, New York, Oxford University Press.

SIMON, ROGER (1982): *Gramsci's Political Thought: An Introduction*, London, Lawrence and Wishart.

SMITH, ROBERT RUTHERFORD (1979): 'Mythic Elements in Television News,' *Journal of Communication*, 29(1) 75–82.

STEEVES, H. LESLIE (1986): *Feminism, Communication and Development: Complementary Goals in the Context of East Africa*, Paper presented at the Conference of the International Association for Mass Communication Research, New Delhi.

THAPAR, ROMILLA (1985): 'Syndicated Moksha,' *Seminar*, 313, September.

THE TIMES OF INDIA (1988): 17 August.

——— (1989): 19 July.

TRACEY, MICHAEL (1985): 'The Poisoned Chalice,' *Daedalus*, Fall.

TUCHMAN, GAYE (1983): 'Consciousness Industries and the Production of Culture,' *Journal of Communication*, 33(3): 26–38.

——— (1978): *Making News: A Study in the Construction of Reality*, New York, Free Press.

WHITE, ROBERT A. (1983): 'Mass Communication and Culture: Transition to a New Paradigm,' *Journal of Communication*, 33(3): 279–301.

WILLIAMS, TANNIS et al. (1986): *The Portrayal of Sex Roles on Canadian and U.S. Television*, Paper presented at the Conference of the International Association for Mass Communication Research, New Delhi.

WORKING GROUP ON SOFTWARE FOR DOORDARSHAN–JOSHI COMMITTEE REPORT (1985): *All Indian Personality for Television*, New Delhi, Publications Division, Ministry of Information and Broadcasting, Government of India.

WOOLLACOTT, JANET (1982): 'Messages and Meanings,' In M. Gurevitch, et al. (eds.), *Culture, Society and the Media*, London, Methuen.

ZOONEN, LIESBET (1986): *Rethinking Women and the News*. Paper presented at the Conference of the International Association for Mass Communication Research, New Delhi.